THIS
IS
ROCKET
SCIENCE

THIS IS ROCK

ET SCIENCE

TRUE STORIES

OF THE

RISK-TAKING

SCIENTISTS

WHO FIGURE

OUT WAYS

TO EXPLORE

BEYOND EARTH

by gloria skurzynski

NATIONAL
GEOGRAPHIC
WASHINGTON, D.C.

FOR MEGAN ALANE GLORIA LEDESMA, WHO WILL LIVE IN A WHOLE NEW WORLD — GS

PUBLISHED BY THE NATIONAL GEOGRAPHIC SOCIETY

John M. Fahey, Jr.,
President & Chief Executive Officer

Gilbert M. Grosvenor,
Chairman of the Board

Tim T. Kelly,
President, Global Media Group

John Q. Griffin,
*Executive Vice President;
President, Publishing*

Nina D. Hoffman,
*Executive Vice President;
President, Book Publishing Group*

Melina Gerosa Bellows,
*Executive Vice President, Children's
Publishing*

PREPARED BY THE BOOK DIVISION

Nancy Laties Feresten,
*Vice President, Editor in Chief,
Children's Books*

Jonathan Halling,
*Design Director,
Children's Publishing*

Jennifer Emmett,
*Executive Editor, Reference &
Solo Titles, Children's Books*

Carl Mehler,
Director of Maps

R. Gary Colbert,
Production Director

Jennifer A. Thornton,
Managing Editor

STAFF FOR THIS BOOK

Suzanne Fonda,
Project Editor

David M. Seager,
Art Director

Lori Epstein, Gloria Skurzynski,
Illustrations Editors

Priyanka Lamichhane,
Associate Editor

Grace Hill,
Associate Managing Editor

Lewis R. Bassford,
Production Manager

Susan Borke,
Legal and Business Affairs

Manufacturing and Quality Management

Christopher A. Liedel,
Chief Financial Officer

Phillip L. Schlosser,
Vice President

Chris Brown,
Technical Director

Nicole Elliott, *Manager*

Rachel Faulise, *Manager*

The National Geographic Society is one of the world's largest nonprofit scientific and educational organizations. Founded in 1888 to "increase and diffuse geographic knowledge," the Society works to inspire people to care about the planet. It reaches more than 325 million people worldwide each month through its official journal, *National Geographic*, and other magazines; National Geographic Channel; television documentaries; music; radio; films; books; DVDs; maps; exhibitions; school publishing programs; interactive media; and merchandise. National Geographic has funded more than 9,000 scientific research, conservation and exploration projects and supports an education program combating geographic illiteracy. For more information, visit nationalgeographic.com.

For more information, please call 1-800-NGS LINE (647-5463) or write to the following address:

National Geographic Society
1145 17th Street N.W.
Washington, D.C. 20036-4688 U.S.A.

Visit us online at www.nationalgeographic.com/books

For librarians and teachers:
www.ngchildrensbooks.org

More for kids from National Geographic:
kids.nationalgeographic.com

For information about special discounts for bulk purchases, please contact National Geographic Books Special Sales: ngspecsales@ngs.org

For rights or permissions inquiries, please contact National Geographic Books Subsidiary Rights: ngbookrights@ngs.org

Skurzynski, Gloria.
 This is rocket science : true stories of the risk-taking scientists who figure out ways to explore beyond Earth / by Gloria Skurzynski.
  p. cm.
 Includes bibliographical references and index.
 ISBN 978-1-4263-0597-9 (hardcover : alk. paper)
 ISBN 978-1-4263-0598-6 (library binding : alk. paper)
 1. Rocketry—Biography. 2. Aerospace engineers—Biography—Juvenile literature. 3. Rocketry—History—Juvenile literature. 4. Rockets (Aeronautics)—History—Juvenile literature. I. Title.
 TL781.85.A1S58 2010
 629.4092'2—dc22
                                    2009020386

Printed in China
09/RRDS/1

Cover: Liftoff of *Dawn* from the Kennedy Space Center
Full Title Page: Imagined spacecraft races into space

ACKNOWLEDGMENTS

The author is exceedingly grateful to rocket scientist Ed Skurzynski and to dedicated editor Suzanne Patrick Fonda and art director David Seager for their continuous support. Deep thanks also to Françoise Ulam; to David S. Nolan; Marc Rayman at NASA Jet Propulsion Laboratory; Mike Wright and Betty Humphery at NASA Marshall Space Flight Center; Norman Chaffee, Roger Weiss, and Mike Gentry at NASA Johnson Space Center; Gwen Pitman at NASA Media Services; Linda S. Sandoval at Los Alamos National Laboratory; Suzanne DuBeau Rostek at Astrotech Space Operations, Inc; Valerie-Anne Lutz van Ammers at the American Philosophical Society Library; Andrew Ilin at Ad Astra; Roger G. Gilbertson at SpaceX; Jordin Kare at Laser-Motive; and, for her continuing inspiration to students, to France Anne Cordova, President of Purdue University and former NASA Chief Scientist, the youngest person and first woman to hold that position.

CONTENTS

FIRE ARROWS 1

Some inventions happen by accident. Two thousand years ago, Chinese scientists searched for a way to make people immortal. They mixed chemicals with liquids and drank them, hoping this would keep them alive forever. Instead, they often died quickly because their experiments contained poisons.

One of the main ingredients in those potions was saltpeter, a potassium nitrate compound found in dry caves in southern China. Alchemists (the scientists searching for eternal life) used saltpeter to dissolve ores and minerals. They learned how to make pure sulfur by heating iron pyrite, also known as fool's gold. And they could easily obtain carbon from coal or charcoal. During centuries of experimentation, the alchemists discovered that if saltpeter, sulfur, and carbon were combined, the mixture would burn.

By A.D. 1040 a Chinese official described three combinations of these ingredients to make three different kinds of weapons: a poison-smoke ball, a bomb that burned, and a bomb that exploded—but not

IN THE 13TH CENTURY THE CHINESE DESIGNED FIRE ARROWS TO USE AS WEAPONS AGAINST INVADING MONGOL ARMIES.

violently. Later experiments showed that when extra saltpeter was added to the three main ingredients, the combination exploded with greater force. This became the earliest form of gunpowder, named *huo yao*, meaning "flaming medicine."

Hollow bamboo tubes filled with this early kind of gunpowder exploded spectacularly when thrown into a fire. These were the first fireworks. Chinese

AT FIRST, FIRE ARROWS FRIGHTENED MONGOL INVADERS AND TERRIFIED THEIR HORSES. THEN THE SOLDIERS LEARNED TO USE FIRE ARROWS AGAINST THEIR OWN ENEMIES.

experimenters attached arrows to these tubes, sealed the tubes at one end, and left the tubes open at the other end. When the gunpowder was lit, a mixture of fire, smoke, and gas flew out through the open end and propelled the weapon forward. Called fire arrows, these weapons weren't accurate enough to hit their targets very often, but their loud explosions frightened enemies. Chinese crossbowmen could shoot the arrows as far as 650 feet.

To the north of China lived nomadic tribes that moved their herds over vast distances of unbroken deserts and grasslands. Many of these tribes united to form the Mongol Empire under the command of the famous Genghis Khan. In A.D. 1232 an army of 30,000 Mongol warriors invaded the Chinese city of Kai-fung-fu, where the Chinese fought back with fire arrows. A book about this battle describes the destruction caused by a single fire arrow: "When it was lit, it made a noise that resembled thunder and extended [about 15 miles]. The place where it fell was burned, and the fire reached more than 2000 feet....These iron nozzles, the flying powder halberds that were hurled, were what the Mongols feared most." The explosions especially terrified the horses. Mongol leaders learned from their enemies and found ways to make fire arrows even more deadly as their invasion spread toward Europe.

On Christmas Day 1241 Mongol troops used fire arrows to capture the city of Budapest in Hungary, and in 1258 to capture the city of Baghdad in what's now Iraq. Soon the Arabs in Baghdad created their own fire arrows and used them against the army of French king Louis IX.

CHINESE CHARACTERS FOR "ROCKET" AND "FIRE ARROW"

AS THE MONGOL CONQUERORS MOVED WEST INTO THE ARAB WORLD, PEOPLE THERE LEARNED TO MAKE THEIR OWN FIRE ARROWS.

By 1300 these weapons had moved farther into Europe, reaching Italy by 1500. There, the people enjoyed exploding them for the same reason the Chinese had at first: to make fireworks. In the old Italian language *rocce* was the word for a long, thin tube. As fire arrows advanced into explosive devices using tubes of iron filled with gunpowder, the word "rocce" evolved into the word "rocket."

Nearly two centuries after the Italians coined the term that became the English word "rocket," British scientist Sir Isaac Newton formulated his famous laws of gravity and motion, now frequently used to explain how rockets and propulsion work. This statue (left) shows Newton standing above an apple. Tradition says that seeing an apple fall from a tree inspired his thoughts about gravity. Newton also built on the ideas of scientists who had come before him—Copernicus, Galileo, and Kepler—to formulate the three laws of motion. He published them in 1687 in a book titled *Philosophiæ Naturalis Principia Mathematica (Mathematical Principles of Natural Philosophy).*

Newton's first law states, "Every object persists in its state of rest or uniform motion in a straight line unless it is compelled to change that state by forces acting upon it." In other words, if something isn't moving, it will stay where it is until something moves it. And if it's moving, it will keep moving at the same speed and in the same direction unless a force acts upon it to change its speed or direction.

What are the forces in Newton's first law as it applies to rockets? Gravity is a force. From the first millisecond of launch, Earth's gravity pulls on the rocket. The force of gravity between two objects depends on the masses of the two objects and the distance between the centers of mass of the two objects. As the distance between two objects gets larger—for example, the distance between Earth and a moving rocket—the gravitational force between them gets smaller.

Thrust is a force caused by hot gases coming out of the rocket that are counteracting the force of gravity and pushing upward against another force: air resistance. These three forces work together, acting on the rocket at launch and during flight.

Newton's second law says, "Force equals mass multiplied by acceleration." As one rocket scientist says, "It's a ridiculously simple and at the same time complex equation." Mass is the amount of matter in an object. Weight is the gravitational attraction of the mass, and the weight stays constant unless the force of gravity is changing. Acceleration is the rate of change in the velocity (speed) of a moving body—a measure of how fast the object is changing its speed.

Thrust in a rocket depends on the rate at which the mass of the burning fuel inside the rocket is expelled through the nozzle at the end of the rocket and the speed at which it escapes. The force of the extremely hot gases escaping through the nozzle accelerates the rocket. The heavier the rocket, the more thrust/force will be needed to move it. If a rocket weighs a million pounds and only a million pounds of thrust is produced, the rocket won't move. To launch it off the ground requires a thrust greater than a million pounds so it can overcome gravity and air resistance. To increase the thrust level requires burning more fuel, using a higher-energy fuel, or both.

Newton's third law reads, "For every action there is an equal and opposite reaction." With rockets, the action is the expelling of high-speed exhaust through the back end. The reaction is the movement of the rocket in the opposite direction. The same thing happens when you blow up a balloon and let it go. The air rushing out of the open end shoots the balloon away from you.

After Newton published his laws of motion, people began to think of rocketry as a science, which of course

TO ESCAPE EARTH
A VEHICLE MUST TRAVEL AT LEAST
SEVEN MILES PER SECOND.

it had been all along. In the 1700s Germans and Russians experimented with rockets so powerful that, when lit and fired, their blasts blew holes in the ground. Gradually, as they understood and applied Newton's laws of motion, scientists began to understand the forces in rocketry—how to control them and what to expect.

DURING THE WAR OF 1812, AS BRITISH WARSHIPS FIRED ROCKETS ON FORT MCHENRY IN MARYLAND, FRANCIS SCOTT KEY WROTE ABOUT "THE ROCKETS' RED GLARE."

Just before the beginning of the 20th century, black powder (gunpowder) rockets had lost most of their importance as weapons. But a better kind of rocket fuel was coming: the vision of three men who would be known as the Fathers of Modern Rocketry.

THE FATHERS OF MODERN ROCKETRY

2

orn in 1857, Konstantin Tsiolkovsky was one of 18 children of a Polish patriot who'd been deported to Russia. When Konstantin was ten years old, he became deaf from scarlet fever. This kept him out of school, but he taught himself by studying as many books as he could borrow, including *From the Earth to the Moon,* the science-based imaginative space-travel adventure by French author Jules Verne. This novel was published at about the time young Konstantin learned to read.

Impressed by his enthusiasm for learning, Konstantin's family sent him to Moscow when he was 16. There, a teacher, who also recognized the boy's brilliance, tutored him at a library every day for three years. Tsiolkovsky not only studied mathematics and science but also became intrigued by rockets.

Later he recalled, "For a long time I thought of the rocket as everybody else did—just as a means of diversion and of petty everyday uses. I do not remember exactly what prompted me to make calculations of its motions. Probably the first seeds of the idea were

H. G. WELLS'S NOVEL *THE WAR OF THE WORLDS* INSPIRED YOUNG FUTURE SCIENTISTS TO DREAM OF SPACE TRAVEL.

sown by that great fantastic author Jules Verne—he directed my thought along certain channels, then came a desire, and after that, the work." As early as 1865, when *From the Earth to the Moon* was published, Jules Verne already knew that escaping Earth's gravity would require great speed. Tsiolkovsky began to think of ways to go fast enough to leave Earth behind. "Earth is the cradle of humanity," he said, "but humanity cannot remain in the cradle forever."

KONSTANTIN TSIOLKOVSKY

At the age of 21 Tsiolkovsky took a job as a math teacher in a small town south of Moscow, where he began to develop his ideas about space flight—not only how to blast rockets off the ground, but also how they could carry humans into space. He wrote scientific articles and several decades later published one titled "The Exploration of Cosmic Space by Means of Reaction Devices." It encouraged readers to "[v]isualize...an elongated metal chamber...designed to protect not only the various physical instruments but also a human pilot....The chamber is partly occupied by a large store of substances which, on being mixed, immediately form an explosive mass."

Tsiolkovsky knew that the speed at which gas escapes from a rocket—called its exhaust velocity—results from the explosive force of the rocket fuel. The more powerful the explosion, the greater the thrust. The propellant mixture Tsiolkovsky had in mind was liquid oxygen (LOX) combined with liquid hydrogen (LH_2), since LH_2 provides high energy per pound.

Halfway around the world, just four years before Tsiolkovsky published his "Reaction Devices" article, 17-year-old Robert Hutchings Goddard climbed a cherry tree behind the barn of his Massachusetts home. A year

THE FIRST ATV*

TO REACH THE INTERNATIONAL SPACE STATION WAS NAMED AFTER FRENCH SCIENCE-FICTION AUTHOR JULES VERNE.

*automated transfer vehicle

ROBERT GODDARD BELIEVED THAT LIQUID-FUEL ROCKETS COULD FLY AS FAR AS THE MOON.

earlier, in 1898, Goddard had read H. G. Wells's science fiction novel *The War of the Worlds*. Perhaps its scenes about invaders from Mars lingered in his mind, because he later wrote that on that day, "I imagined how wonderful it would be to make some device which had even the possibility of ascending to Mars, and how it would look... if sent up from the meadow at my feet...."

At Clark University Robert Goddard received a Ph.D. in physics and set up an experiment to prove that rockets could fly in a vacuum, which most people doubted. He built a chamber, removed all the air from it, put a small rocket inside, and fired it. This experiment convinced him that rockets could not only fly in a vacuum, but also achieve up to 20 percent more thrust in a vacuum than in air because there was no air resistance to reduce the rocket's thrust.

Goddard had ideas about fuel, too. Unaware of Tsiolkovsky's article, Goddard believed that liquid propellant was a higher-energy fuel that created more thrust than solid propellant did. In solid-fuel rockets the grain (the propellant charge) is densely packed and molded inside a casing. Goddard understood the disadvantages of liquid propellants—they're harder to handle than solid propellants like gunpowder. Also, the two components, fuel and oxidizer, have to be kept in separate tanks until launch, and liquid oxygen (the oxidizer) must be stored at a very low temperature, near −300°F. But the advantage of liquid propellants is that during flight, the rate at which they're injected into the combustion chamber can be increased or decreased or shut off if necessary, while solid fuels burn until they're completely used up. Goddard would have liked to combine LH_2 with LOX, but LH_2 was hard to come by. Instead, he used gasoline combined with LOX for his rocket experiments.

In 1920 Goddard published a paper titled "A Method for Reaching Extreme Altitudes." It claimed that if a rocket was large enough and had fuel that was powerful enough, it could reach the Moon. The press ignores most academic papers, but the *New York Times* happened to see this one and responded by ridiculing Dr. Goddard's theory about flights in a vacuum. The *Times* insisted that space travel was impossible because unless a rocket had an atmosphere to push against, it couldn't move at all: "That Professor Goddard...does not know the relation of action to reaction, and of the need to have something better than a vacuum against which to react—to say that [about reaching the Moon] would be absurd. [He] seems to lack the knowledge ladled out daily in high schools." It didn't matter that the *New York Times* was wrong and Goddard was right; Goddard felt humiliated. He moved to New Mexico and continued his rocket research away from the public eye.

Across the Atlantic a young scientist tried to recover from Germany's defeat in World War I. Like Tsiolkovsky,

"PROFESSOR GODDARD... SEEMS TO LACK THE KNOWLEDGE LADLED OUT DAILY IN HIGH SCHOOLS."

NEW YORK TIMES

Hermann Oberth had been fascinated as a boy by Jules Verne's novel *From the Earth to the Moon.* He said later that he'd read it "at least five or six times and, finally, knew [it] by heart." Oberth realized that some of Verne's ideas were not just science fiction, but real science. At age 14 Oberth designed a model rocket. He had no way to test it, but he delved into mathematics to teach himself propulsion theories.

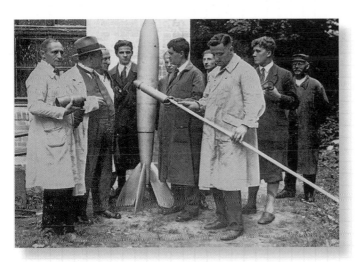

After the war Oberth studied physics. In 1923 he wrote a paper called "By Rocket into Planetary Space," and in 1929, in a longer version of the paper, he forecast "rockets...so [powerful] that they could be capable of carrying a man aloft." In a footnote Oberth mentioned Goddard's "A Method for Reaching Extreme Altitudes."

PROFESSOR HERMANN OBERTH, (TO THE RIGHT OF THE LARGE ROCKET), GATHERS MEMBERS OF HIS DESIGN TEAM FOR A TEST FIRING. STUDENT WERNHER VON BRAUN IS SECOND FROM RIGHT.

Russia not only had lived through World War I but also had survived a turbulent revolution that increased its territory and gave rise to a new name: Union of Soviet Socialist Republics, or Soviet Union for short. When the Soviet newspaper *Izvestia* mentioned Oberth's publication, Tsiolkovsky read it and saw the reference to Goddard's work, which he hadn't heard about. Tsiolkovsky decided to republish his own early articles about space travel and include with them a number of his newer theories.

These three scientists have been called the Fathers

These three scientists have been called the Fathers of Modern Rocketry. They never met and at first were unaware of each others' ideas about rocket propulsion, yet they independently came to pretty much the same conclusions. All believed in the superiority of liquid fuels for rocket propulsion. Their research on liquid propellants inspired two men who would become key players in the 1950s space race between two superpowers.

Not long after Oberth wrote his "Planetary Space" paper, 13-year-old Wernher von Braun tied six skyrockets to a toy wagon and lit them. Belching smoke and flame, the little red wagon roared five blocks through a crowded Berlin street and then exploded. In the uproar that followed, police grabbed the boy and kept him in the police station until his furious father came to get him out.

WERNHER VON BRAUN

His father's anger didn't put an end to von Braun's fascination with rockets. Like so many other budding rocket scientists, he'd read the science fiction of Jules Verne and H. G. Wells. But he'd also read Oberth's paper, which inspired him to learn calculus and trigonometry so he could understand the physics of rocketry. Later, as von Braun studied for his Ph.D. at the University of Berlin, he worked as an assistant to Professor Oberth, and in 1932 von Braun and a few other men began designing liquid-fuel rockets for the German military.

In 1936 von Braun became technical director of Germany's military rocket program. Soon, he and his team launched two liquid-fuel rockets that went a mile and a half high. Shortly after that, the Soviets, who'd also been working with liquid propulsion, fired a rocket that soared more than eight miles into the sky. And a month later, one of Robert Goddard's rockets flew faster than the speed of sound. Von Braun and his team read about this in journals and used some of Goddard's ideas in their own designs.

During World War II German military commanders, under the rule of Adolf Hitler, wanted to use rockets as deadly weapons of war—military missiles that could deliver explosive warheads onto enemy territory.

As has been true with all other rockets since the first fire arrows, no one person can be credited with the entire design of the German rocket. Tsiolkovsky, Oberth, and others had envisioned elements of this kind of rocket. Goddard had already launched his own version of a liquid-fuel rocket. Von Braun and his fellow rocket scientists worked at developing theirs at a facility named Peenemunde. As the war went on, it was hard for von Braun and his crew to find petroleum products, but German farms were producing bumper crops of potatoes. Potatoes can be distilled into ethyl alcohol. By combining ethyl alcohol with liquid oxygen, the German "Rocket Team" had what they needed. By 1944 they'd nearly perfected the deadly Vengeance Weapon 2 rocket, shortened to V-2. It had a 200-mile range and carried a 2-ton warhead.

In his 2007 book *Red Moon Rising,* journalist Matthew Brzezinski describes in detail the launch of a V-2 from the German-occupied Dutch coast. He writes, "Twenty-five seconds had elapsed since liftoff. During that period, the rocket had shed six thousand pounds." That's 6,000 pounds of liquid propellant burned off and converted into thrust. "At an altitude of seventeen miles, the turbine shut down, cutting off fuel to the combustion chamber. Now the rocket was a projectile, a forty-six-foot-long

THE V-2 ROCKET WAS BUILT AND TESTED AT A GERMAN FACILITY CALLED PEENEMUNDE.

That V-2 rocket reached an altitude of 52 miles before gravity curved it downward to eventually land with a tremendous explosion in London. By the end of the war, of the almost 6,000 V-2 rockets the Germans had built, 3,500 had been launched—40 percent of them aimed at England. The damage was ruinous.

When the war neared its final days, the United States and the Soviet Union both wanted the designs for the V-2 rockets as well as the engineers who'd built them. Entering Germany with their invading armies, Soviet and American intelligence teams began searching through German installations for any V-2 parts and engineers they could find. The Soviet team included Sergei Korolev.

THE BRITISH MINISTRY OF DEFENSE ASSURED CITIZENS THEY'D BE PROTECTED FROM THE DEADLY V-2. POSTERS SUCH AS THIS ONE HELPED TO CALM FEARS.

As a teenager Korolev had spent hours watching seaplanes and gliders at a naval airstrip near his home in Odessa, a major port in the Soviet Republic of Ukraine. The pilots grew so used to young Korolev hanging around that they let him work on the planes and even took him for flights. At 17 Korolev joined an amateur aircraft club and later entered college to study aeronautical engineering. After graduation he joined GIRD, a Soviet research group working on rocket propulsion.

Then came horrible times for Korolev. In 1938, in a political purge ordered by the leader of the Soviet Union, Josef Stalin, Korolev was accused of "subversion in a new field of technology" and was sent to concentration camps in Siberia, where he nearly died from beatings and starvation. Later, the Soviets realized the value of his expertise and transferred him to a prison where he could continue his rocket research. In 1944, after he'd gathered V-2 information in Germany, he returned to Moscow and began to design military missiles based on the German rockets. But he was more interested in developing rockets for space travel than for warfare. About one of his designs he said angrily, "The purpose of this rocket is to get *there!* [He pointed to the sky.] This is not some military toy!"

The German technology that Korolev and the other Soviets recovered couldn't compare with the gift that the United States received two days after Hitler committed suicide in Berlin. On May 2, 1945, a young German on a bicycle rode up to a U.S. Army infantry private on patrol in the Bavarian Alps. The bicyclist called out, "My name is Magnus von Braun. My brother invented the V-2. We want to surrender."

WITH HIS ARM IN A CAST, WERNHER VON BRAUN SURRENDERED TO U.S. ARMY AGENTS IN APRIL 1945. HIS BROTHER MAGNUS STANDS TO HIS RIGHT.

Wernher von Braun, his left arm in a cast, gave himself up to the Yankees. Along with more than a hundred other German rocket scientists, he was taken first to White Sands, New Mexico, not far from where Robert Goddard had been launching his experimental rockets.

Von Braun later said that Goddard's rockets may have been "rather crude by present-day standards, but they blazed the trail" for modern rockets and space vehicles.

peration Paperclip. That was the code name for the relocation of German rocket engineers to the United States, because each of their files was marked by a paperclip. In 1946 Wernher von Braun and 120 other men from the German Rocket Team were transported to the missile proving ground near Fort Bliss, Texas, close to the Mexican border.

Sixty of their V-2 rockets had been brought from Germany, but even though von Braun had ideas for improving them, his requests for new material were denied. He couldn't even get linoleum to cover the cracks in the floor of his lab. As for the possibility of sending a rocket into orbit?—forget it! The U.S. government had other priorities and other worries. Germany surrendered to the United States and its allies on May 7, 1945, but the war continued in the Pacific. Japan didn't concede defeat until American aircraft dropped atomic bombs on two Japanese cities in the summer of 1945. Victory made the U.S. feel secure in its military superiority...until the Soviet Union detonated its first atomic bomb in 1949. That meant that now two countries—

THE WORLD WATCHED AND LISTENED WITH AMAZED EXCITEMENT AS SPUTNIK (SHOWN HERE IN ARTWORK) CIRCLED EARTH.

the United States and the Soviet Union—were equal in their destructive power. The two superpowers and their allies were in a cold war—a nuclear standoff—that could turn into a hot war with drastic consequences. The U.S. government decided to pour billions of dollars into building up its bomber fleet, especially long-range bombers that could reach the Soviet Union, rather than relying on guided missiles.

There's a difference between a rocket and a guided missile. A rocket doesn't carry its own guidance system. It has to be fired in the direction it's supposed to go. A guided missile is a rocket-propelled weapon with a warhead and a guidance system that directs it to a target, like the V-2s the Germans had built.

The U.S. military considered guided missiles less effective than bombers because they couldn't travel as far. Still, they might have some usefulness. Wernher von Braun and members of his team were transferred to Redstone Arsenal in Huntsville, Alabama, where, with American engineers and military personnel, they developed the Redstone ballistic missile, based on V-2 technology. Sixty-nine feet long, the Redstone burned alcohol and liquid oxygen and produced about 75,000 pounds of thrust. It was one of the first American guided missiles that could carry an atomic bomb, but it could fly no farther than 400 miles.

Meanwhile, the Soviet Union didn't have the financial resources to build hundreds of bombers to keep up with America's growing aircraft arsenal. It did, though, have the V-2 documentation taken from Germany and the expertise of rocket scientist Sergei Korolev. With the blessings of the Soviet government, Korolev began to

JUST SIX MONTHS AFTER ITS FIRST SUCCESSFUL FLIGHT, AN R-7 LIKE THIS ONE LAUNCHED SPUTNIK INTO ORBIT AROUND EARTH.

design a missile that could lift 276 tons and carry a 3-ton nuclear warhead as far as 7,456 miles—more than enough to reach the United States. (The distance from Moscow to New York City is 4,681 miles.) Named the R-7, the Soviet missile used kerosene and liquid oxygen for fuel and was first successfully launched on August 21, 1957.

The R-7 all liquid-fuel rocket included four strap-on booster rockets, each with its own propellant tank. After the boosters ignited and achieved thrust, the five stacked stages of the central rocket ignited one after the other, and the missile rose. At a certain altitude the boosters separated and fell back toward Earth. When the Soviets announced the launch of their "super long-distance intercontinental multistage ballistic missile," the rest of the world, thinking it was just a propaganda claim, didn't pay much attention—until October 4. Then the whole world became electrified!

On that day an R-7 rocket lofted Sputnik, the first artificial satellite, into orbit around Earth. Every hour and 35 minutes Sputnik sped around Earth, at a speed of 18,000 miles per hour and an altitude of 560 miles. Twenty-two inches in diameter, with 4 antennae sticking out at angles, the beeping satellite weighed 184 pounds and sent out signals that could be picked up by amateur radio operators everywhere. Sputnik kept on beeping for 21 days. You can hear its recorded sound at http://www.nytimes.com/partners/aol/special/sputnik/sputnik.au.

Soviet military officials had not been too pleased about Korolev using up their scarce missile resources to send a beeping ball into space. Boris Chertok, one of Sputnik's chief designers, later recalled, "We regarded it as Korolev's little toy! We weren't prepared

for the impact this small ball would have on mankind."
The world's excited reaction to Sputnik at first surprised
the Soviets, then delighted them.

In the United States the reaction was dismay.
Suddenly Americans felt like losers. The country had
been planning to launch its own satellite, but not
anywhere near as heavy as 184 pounds. Sputnik's
size hinted that Soviet rockets were more powerful—
maybe powerful enough to carry a nuclear warhead
all the way to America. Trying to downplay the threat,
President Dwight Eisenhower called Sputnik just
"one small ball in the air" that "does not raise my
apprehensions, not one iota....the mere fact that this
thing orbits involves no new discovery to science." He
added that no additional money would be spent on
the U.S. missile program.

SERGEI KOROLEV WITH LAIKA

That was bad news for rocket scientists, especially
when a month later the Soviets launched a second
satellite. This one had a small cabin that contained a
live passenger: a dog named Laika—a Russian word
meaning "barker." Laika, a little stray who'd been
found on the streets of Moscow, orbited for only four
days before she died when her cabin overheated.
Perhaps that was merciful, because she never would
have survived reentry into Earth's atmosphere.

Trying hard to play catch-up, the U.S. prepared to
launch a satellite of its own. Much smaller than Sputnik,
this satellite weighed only 3.25 pounds and measured
6.4 inches in diameter. It was supposed to be launched
from Cape Canaveral, along Florida's Atlantic coast, and
be carried into space on a three-stage Vanguard rocket
that was 72 feet high and 3 feet, 9 inches, in diameter.

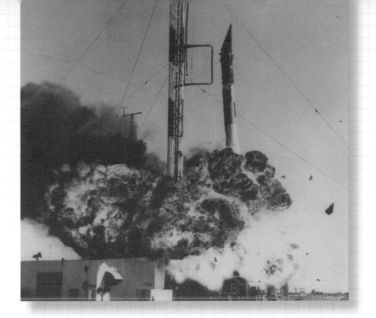

**"IT SANK,
LIKE A GREAT
FLAMING
SWORD
INTO ITS
SCABBARD."**

KURT STEHLING,
HEAD OF THE
VANGUARD
PROPULSION GROUP

Of the three stages, the third burned solid fuel to create a thrust of 3,100 pounds. The second stage would burn liquid fuel for an additional 7,500 pounds of thrust. The first stage, a modified Viking rocket, had a propellant of kerosene and liquid oxygen providing a 28,000-pound thrust at liftoff. Even though the satellite was no bigger than a grapefruit, it needed all that thrust to lift the heavy rocket and to overcome the gravitational pull of Earth at takeoff.

Launch day, December 6, 1957: The Vanguard rocket ignited, rose two feet above the launchpad, and then settled backward onto the pad, fell over, and burst into flames. The first U.S. attempt to launch a satellite had failed alarmingly, although the little satellite itself had been thrown clear, rolling away from the rocket. Its radio transmitter kept beeping until someone finally reached it and turned it off. The press called the failed attempt "Kaputnik."

Desperate for a success, the U.S. government turned to the Redstone Arsenal in Huntsville, Alabama. When propulsion systems are designed for specific missions,

EXPLORER'S ORBIT

225 MILES

EXPLORER **1,594 MILES**

AS EXPLORER ORBITED EARTH, ITS SCIENTIFIC INSTRUMENTS DISCOVERED THE VAN ALLEN RADIATION BELT.

SUCCESS! ON JANUARY 31, 1958, A JUPITER C ROCKET LAUNCHED EXPLORER 1 FROM CAPE CANAVERAL, IN FLORIDA.

the engineers don't start from scratch—if they did, it would take a decade to design and test each new component the countless times needed to make sure everything works right. Instead, they "massage" (engineers' term) existing systems to fill the new criteria and answer questions like these: Depending on what the aerodynamic forces will be, will we need a large motor or small? Solid fuel or liquid? High stress or low stress? Steel or fiberglass cases? Low cost or low maintenance? What are the unknown factors that might come up? (Unknown factors are called "unk-unks," short for "unknown unknowns.") Then, taking available materials and "pushing them together," engineers build what's needed.

Told that the goal was to launch an artificial satellite into Earth's orbit by March 1958, Wernher von Braun and his team added a solid-fuel fourth stage to the Redstone and renamed it the Jupiter. They beat the deadline! On the night of January 31, 1958, Jupiter launched spectacularly, lofting a bullet-shaped satellite called Explorer 1. As Explorer looped around Earth, von Braun declared, "We have firmly established our foothold in space. We will never give it up again."

Years later Boris Chertok, the Russian space engineer quoted on page 27, said, "However unpleasant it might sound, the Cold War stimulated the development of space and satellite technology. If we had lived as peacefully as we do today, we would not have put so much money into space technology development as we did in the latter half of the 20th century."

4

ompetition between the Americans and the Soviets grew intense. Who would reach the Moon first? A big, strong, powerful rocket would be needed to lift a spacecraft beyond Earth orbit, and the Soviets already had the Vostok. In April 1961 a Vostok carried cosmonaut Yuri Gagarin 187 miles high, making one orbit around Earth that lasted 108 minutes. A month later a Redstone rocket lifted astronaut Alan Shepard not quite high enough to attain orbit. Shepard's *Freedom 7* spacecraft reached 116 miles in altitude and returned to Earth after a 15-minute suborbital flight.

That was a good beginning, and other flights followed. Then, on September 12, 1962, President John F. Kennedy declared, "We choose to go to the moon in this decade...because that challenge is one that we are willing to accept, one we are unwilling to postpone, and one which we intend to win."

The program that would attempt to send an American to the Moon was named Apollo. NASA's launch vehicle, the Saturn C-1, continued to be expanded until it grew into the much bigger Saturn V (pronounced

IT HAS BEEN MORE THAN 40 YEARS SINCE THE FIRST U.S. ASTRONAUTS WALKED ON THE MOON IN 1969. TODAY, OTHER NATIONS HOPE TO DUPLICATE THIS FEAT.

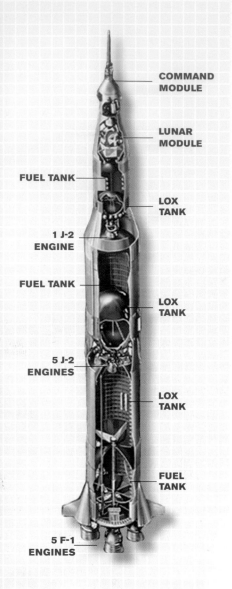

COMMAND
MODULE

LUNAR
MODULE

FUEL TANK

LOX
TANK

1 J-2
ENGINE

FUEL TANK

LOX
TANK

5 J-2
ENGINES

LOX
TANK

FUEL
TANK

5 F-1
ENGINES

THE MIGHTY SATURN V
PROVED POWERFUL ENOUGH
TO CARRY ASTRONAUTS
BEYOND EARTH ORBIT.
WERNHER VON BRAUN
MASTERMINDED THE
ROCKET'S DESIGN.

Saturn five) designed to ferry astronauts on a lunar trip. Including its three stages, the Saturn V stood 363 feet tall and weighed more than 6 million pounds. Developed at NASA's Marshall Space Flight Center in Huntsville, Alabama, under the direction of Wernher von Braun, Saturn V had a first-stage cluster of five F-1 rocket engines, the largest liquid-propellant engines ever built. The total thrust of the Saturn V was 8.7 million pounds!

But a few rocket scientists believed that Saturn V wasn't nearly big enough or powerful enough or ambitious enough to send humans to the Moon and then beyond to the planets—and perhaps, in decades to come, even farther than the edges of the solar system.

Stanislaw Ulam, one of these forward-looking scientists, was born in Lwow, Poland. As a boy Stan read Jules Verne's *From the Earth to the Moon* (another fan!) and remembered "how Jules Verne and H. G. Wells had influenced me in my childhood." Ulam's visionary quest was to propel a spacecraft by using nuclear bombs for propulsion—1,000 bombs on board, ejected one at a time through the rear of the spacecraft, exploding *behind* the craft to push the vessel through space by the force of the explosions. Think of a firecracker blowing up underneath a tin plate and blasting it into the air. Ulam's nuclear propulsion idea would work like that on a gargantuan scale.

Ulam was already working on the atomic bomb at Los Alamos in New Mexico. He shared his idea with fellow scientists Theodore Taylor and Freeman Dyson, who took the project to General Atomics Corporation in San Diego, California. The project's name—Orion—was chosen because the constellation Orion is shaped like "a man in the heavens," and that was their ambition: to send not just one man, but many humans into the heavens. For propulsion the team proposed nuclear-fission bombs, each one smaller than a baseball. The thousand or more bombs would fire rapidly, one following the other a second or less apart as they ejected at the rear of the spacecraft. Thirty feet behind the spacecraft they would explode, and their powerful impacts would hit a "pusher plate" on the rocket. The force of the explosions, following rapidly one after the other on the pusher plate, would be more than enough to propel the spacecraft forward—fast!

The designers built a few models that they named Putt-Putts and Hot Rods, and they managed to stage one small test flight at a place called Jackass Flats, Nevada. In order to continue developing the project, though, they needed funding, and NASA wasn't much interested in their proposal. Instead, NASA was betting on von Braun's big Saturn V, which used chemical propulsion, not nuclear propulsion.

Saturn V couldn't compare in size to the proposed Orion. Orion's base was 185 feet in diameter, and its height was 280 feet. The mass at takeoff would be 10,000 *tons*, and the vehicle could carry a crew of eight or more astronauts, at a time when NASA was planning on just three.

And that was Orion's small version! Planners envisioned an even more massive Orion, one that would weigh eight *million* tons and carry a crew of *150* astronauts to the planet Saturn and back home to Earth in just three years. It would build up speed as it raced through space. The design team's motto was "Mars by 1965, Saturn by 1970." If Orion kept accelerating, in 30 years it would reach a speed of 6.2 miles per second, and in 150 years it would reach Centaurus, our nearest star after the Sun!

It is tempting to call Ulam, Taylor, and Dyson impossible dreamers who imagined a science-fiction universe. They were actually brilliant scientists, physicists, engineers, and mathematicians. But to U.S. government decision-makers, even though Mars might be an inviting target for some year far in the future, the Moon had to come first. That was the real race.

Without money to buy the components, to build the models, and to pay the salaries of the engineers, no project can move forward, and the U.S. government was not at all eager to finance a project that sounded so much like science fiction. Traveling to Mars and back in 125 days with a crew of eight? Unimaginable! Project Orion received barely enough funding to keep the idea limping along for seven years, and during that whole time it was top secret. Hardly anyone knew about it.

In 1963 Stan Ulam, Wernher von Braun, and science-fiction writer Isaac Asimov spoke together at a meeting of the American Nuclear Society (ANS). Von Braun had offered some amount of encouragement to the Orion team, but his own Saturn V was NASA's prime focus and soon would be tested.

Ulam was a Polish Jew whose father, sister, and uncles had been killed by the Nazis during the Holocaust in World War II. In those same years von Braun was overseeing the production of V-2 rockets, which were put together by

PROJECT ORION WAS CALLED "DIRTY" BECAUSE IT REQUIRED NUCLEAR-FISSION FUEL.

concentration-camp inmates. Both men became U.S. citizens. Ulam, who worked on developing top-secret nuclear bomb designs, remained mostly anonymous. In contrast, von Braun was not only visible, he became an icon to the American public.

NUCLEAR-POWERED PROJECT ORION (SHOWN AS ART) PROMISED A ROUND-TRIP TO MARS IN 125 DAYS. STAN ULAM'S IDEAS WERE NEVER TESTED.

The two men had contributed to technologies intended to create destruction in warfare. When Ulam and von Braun came together on that panel at the ANS conference, was their meeting strained, or at least a little strange? Ulam was the first speaker. He said, "Nuclear energy seems—in the near future—to be the most promising,...if not the most immediate way to go beyond the first steps in space, and to guarantee achievements far beyond what has already been accomplished."

Von Braun spoke next. To introduce himself he

announced, "If Dr. Ulam is a mathematical wizard, I am the plumber in the rocket racket, and therefore would like to talk to you in somewhat more specific details on our nuclear rocket program." Later von Braun commented about Ulam's "pulse type nuclear propulsion whereby—ridiculous as it may sound—you push your ship through space by exploding a string of small A-bombs behind its heat-protected tail." Were von Braun's remarks meant to be amusing, or was he criticizing the project? During the rest of the ANS meeting von Braun spoke more approvingly of nuclear propulsion. Yet nuclear propulsion continued to lag behind chemical propulsion in the competition for government funding.

Project Orion's death blow had begun in the same year as the ANS panel meeting, when it was derailed by the Nuclear Test Ban of 1963. The United States, Great Britain, and the Soviet Union signed a treaty prohibiting nuclear tests in space, in the atmosphere, and underwater. Project Orion's nuclear propulsion was never intended to be used as a weapon, but critics claimed that if any of the rocket's nuclear-fission bombs blew up on takeoff, radioactive fallout could harm people on Earth. Ulam disagreed that the fallout would be dangerous, but he supported the test-ban treaty.

Ulam's widow, Françoise Ulam, now in her nineties, lives in Santa Fe, New Mexico, not far from Los Alamos. She recently recalled, "For Stan, Orion meant exploring the universe in a peaceful way. When he was a little child he called himself 'S. Ulam, mathematician, physicist and astronomer.' Since he was so fond of astronomy he really wanted Orion to be for peaceful space exploration and nothing to do with wartime or fighting."

"ORION MEANT EXPLORING THE UNIVERSE IN A PEACEFUL WAY."

FRANÇOISE ULAM

NASA's 1968 budget stated, "Funding for nuclear propulsion research had to compete with funding for the Vietnam War and funding for a multitude of new social programs. In addition, the initial interest that von Braun and other space planners had shown in nuclear propulsion shifted to a single goal—[to meet President] Kennedy's lunar landing mandate. Von Braun and others had to rely on what they knew best—chemical propulsion...." Nuclear propulsion, like other nontraditional propulsion technologies, would have to wait.

STAN ULAM AND EDWARD TELLER SHARED A TITLE BUT DISAGREED ABOUT RESTRICTIONS ON NUCLEAR ENERGY. ULAM FAVORED RESTRICTIONS; TELLER DID NOT.

To NASA, the Saturn V rocket appeared much more reasonable than Project Orion, since Orion was hampered by these political problems concerning nuclear fallout. For that reason Saturn, the chemical rocket, got all the funding it needed. The planets Mars and Saturn were going to have to wait—maybe forever—for human visitors to arrive on nuclear-propelled spaceships. The big push was to get to the Moon, and in that race the rocket Saturn V won and Project Orion lost.

In January 1967 tragedy struck the Apollo space program before the first launch. A fire during a ground test took the lives of three astronauts: Virgil Grissom, Edward White, and Roger Chaffee. Not until 22 months later did the first three-man Apollo-Saturn mission orbit Earth.

Then, on July 16, 1969, the fifth Apollo mission, named Apollo 11, launched from Cape Canaveral atop a Saturn V rocket. The first stage burned for 2.5 minutes,

It's A Wise Father That Knows His Own Bomb

ARMSTRONG
AND
ALDRIN
ATE
COOKIES
AND
PEACHES
ON THE MOON.

lifting the rocket to an altitude of 38 miles. Even after it separated from the rest of the rocket, the first stage continued upward for another 30 miles before gravity pulled it into the Atlantic Ocean. The second stage ignited, burned, separated, and fell back to Earth. The third stage ignited and then shut off as planned. Two and a half hours after launch it reignited, burning for six more minutes as it pushed the module into a trajectory toward the Moon. Thirty minutes after that the third stage separated and fell away from the spacecraft. Astronaut/passenger Neil Armstrong radioed back, "Hey Houston....This Saturn gave us a magnificent ride. It was beautiful." Later, fellow crewman Michael Collins announced, "The Saturn V rocket which put us in [lunar] orbit is an incredibly complicated piece of machinery, every piece of which worked flawlessly."

As Collins piloted *Columbia*, Apollo's lunar orbiter, Armstrong and Edwin "Buzz" Aldrin entered *Eagle*, an exploratory module, and descended to the lunar surface. Armstrong took the first steps on the Moon, telling the world it was "one small step for [a] man; one giant leap for mankind."

All across America families gathered together, eyes riveted to the black-and-white images on their television screens as they watched Armstrong and Aldrin maneuvering awkwardly in their bulky spacesuits on the Moon's surface. Families rushed outside, where fathers lifted the little ones onto their shoulders and pointed to that big, bright, silver disk in the sky. The older kids danced with excitement and dreamed that one day...maybe...

And Americans exulted, "We did it! We won."

BLASTOFF! CAPE CANAVERAL IS A USEFUL LAUNCH SITE BECAUSE IT'S CLOSE TO THE EQUATOR, WHERE EARTH ROTATES FASTER THAN IT DOES NEAR THE POLES. THIS HELPS SPACECRAFT RACE INTO ORBIT.

5

The Saturn V, the largest and most powerful rocket ever built, would carry astronauts to the Moon five more times: Apollo 17 was the final lunar mission, ending in 1972. For Americans the space race was pretty much finished after the Moon landing. A NASA publication titled *Suddenly, Tomorrow Came* asked, "Where do we go from here? Or why should we go anywhere?" It continued, "By the close of 1972 the United States had launched 27 manned spacecraft into space and returned them safely to Earth. 34 individuals had traveled in space, 17 of them more than once; and 12 had walked on the Moon. Eleven three-man Apollo flights were launched. The race was over. America had won."

So what next? Slowly a new idea began to take shape. Maybe NASA could build space stations stretching from low Earth orbit all the way to the Moon. One by one, the stations would be launched from Earth by the massive Saturn V rockets. Astronauts could be transported into orbit and back to Earth in a two-stage, reusable space plane with wings. Like an airplane, it would take off and land on solid earth instead of splashing

THE SPACE SHUTTLE WAS DESIGNED TO LAUNCH LIKE A ROCKET, ORBIT LIKE A SPACECRAFT, AND LAND LIKE AN AIRPLANE. IT ACCOMPLISHED ALL THREE.

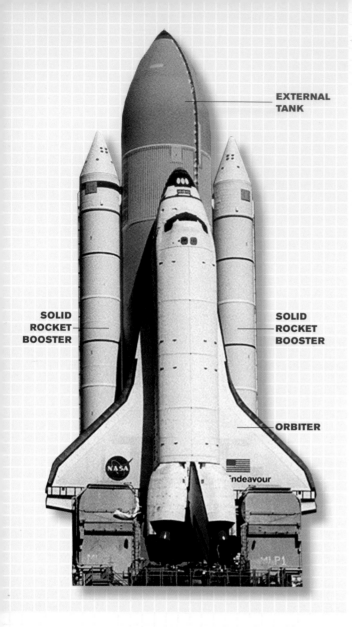

EXTERNAL
TANK

SOLID
ROCKET
BOOSTER

SOLID
ROCKET
BOOSTER

ORBITER

THE ORBITER AND THE
SOLID ROCKET BOOSTERS
FLY MORE THAN ONCE. THE
EXTERNAL TANK BURNS UP
AFTER EACH LAUNCH.

down in an ocean. This new spacecraft would be called the Space Transportation System (STS), or, more commonly, the space shuttle. It would be so powerful and so inexpensive to operate that eventually it could launch as many as 50 times a year.

That was NASA's vision in 1972. In reality, it was ten years before the space shuttle made its first launch and ten more years before it made its 50th flight.

Working for more than a decade, NASA engineers designed, redesigned, and rebuilt the model for the shuttle, and still it was just a model. The actual spacecraft would have three parts: the orbiter (the part that looks like an airplane), a huge external tank (ET) filled with liquid fuel, and two solid-fuel rocket boosters (SRBs).

Funds dwindled as public enthusiasm for space exploration began to shrink. "All of a sudden we had to lay people off," a NASA director recalled. It was mostly the youngest and newest engineers who lost their jobs because of budget cuts. The experienced aerospace engineers who remained were devoted to their work, staying on the job far longer than 40 hours a week. Another director said, "They understood the necessity to test their theories. They often worked in crummy offices but had very fine laboratories." Each employee at NASA had to be a doer, not just a watcher.

Building the massive space vehicle was a design

responsibility that couldn't be hurried. Every detail was important and vital to the safety of the astronauts who would travel in it. The shuttle was designed to launch like a rocket, orbit like a spacecraft, and land like a glider. It was the first spacecraft with wings and the first spacecraft designed to be used over and over again. That meant its thermal (heat) protection had to last through repeated flights. A task force of NASA engineers developed a special kind of tile to insulate the wing edge of the shuttle to protect it from the extreme heat of reentry. It took a lot of tries. Next, they had to develop new adhesives strong enough to stick tiles to the wing and belly surfaces. They tested several before they found one that worked best. Each of the 31,000 tiles on the wings, bottom, and sides of the first shuttle was carefully crafted and then glued on by hand, one at a time. For the shuttle *Columbia,* the first one to fly, this tile shielding required 670,000 hours of labor. That amounts to 335 man *years* not man hours of labor. ("Man hours" and "man years" are terms used in the science of statistics. Both terms include work done by women.)

The design and redesign continued until a finished vehicle at last stood tall and powerful. The original orbiter was supposed to be named *Constitution,* but fans of the *Star Trek* television series began a letter-writing campaign that persuaded President Gerald Ford to call it *Enterprise* after the *Star Trek* ship. *Enterprise,* built as a test vehicle for training

GASES
IN A
SOLID-FUEL ROCKET
MOTOR ARE
6100°F—
HOT ENOUGH TO
BOIL
STEEL!

flights, never reached orbit. It's now on exhibit at the Smithsonian Institution's Steven F. Udvar-Hazy Center, in Chantilly, Virginia. The shuttles that would fly into space were christened *Columbia*, *Challenger*, *Discovery*, *Atlantis,* and *Endeavour.* Problems with the main engine and the heat protection tiles on *Columbia* slowed progress. At last, in 1981, two years behind schedule and one billion dollars over budget because of the intense focus on safety and reliability, *Columbia* became the first space shuttle to reach Earth orbit.

The space shuttle is one of the most complicated pieces of machinery ever built and the first piloted spacecraft to use solid-fuel booster rockets, which are fished out of the ocean, cleaned out, rebuilt, and refilled after every flight. Before the next flight each shuttle has to be thoroughly examined, repaired, and reconstructed to make sure it is safe to fly again. The reusability of the shuttle sets it apart from the Soyuz, its Russian counterpart.

The Russian Soyuz are the most frequently used launch rockets in the world. The name "Soyuz" is also used for the crew capsules and cargo capsules carried by the launch rockets. Powered by kerosene and liquid oxygen that together produce 907,000 pounds of thrust to lift a total weight of 639,000 pounds, Soyuz launch rockets cannot be used more than once. Each *Soyuz* capsule atop a rocket makes only one trip into space— and back, if it's carrying a crew. If it's carrying just cargo, the capsule delivers its freight and then burns up from the heat of atmospheric drag as it reenters Earth's atmosphere. A *Soyuz* crew capsule, which is slowed by parachutes before landing, can get a bit battered when it hits the ground. None of them is reused.

A WORKER ATTACHES ONE OF THE MAIN ENGINES TO A SHUTTLE INSIDE THE ORBITER PROCESSING FACILITY AT KENNEDY SPACE CENTER.

A shuttle's three cone-shaped main engines are mounted at the tail end of the orbiter. Each engine produces 375,000 pounds of thrust. At liftoff these engines ignite first, burning their LOX and LH_2 fuel at the rate of half a ton per second, followed almost immediately by ignition of the solid rocket boosters and the external tank.

These rocket boosters are the largest solid propellant rockets ever flown. They're filled with an oxidizer called ammonium perchlorate combined with aluminum, iron oxide, and a binder to hold the mixture together. The ingredients are molded into solid form and packed inside half-inch-thick metal shell casings. At launch each solid rocket booster burns for approximately 123 seconds and creates thrust averaging 2.6 million pounds.

The external tank (ET) holds 143,000 gallons of LOX and 383,000 gallons of LH_2 in separate tanks. The tank is covered with inch-thick foam insulation

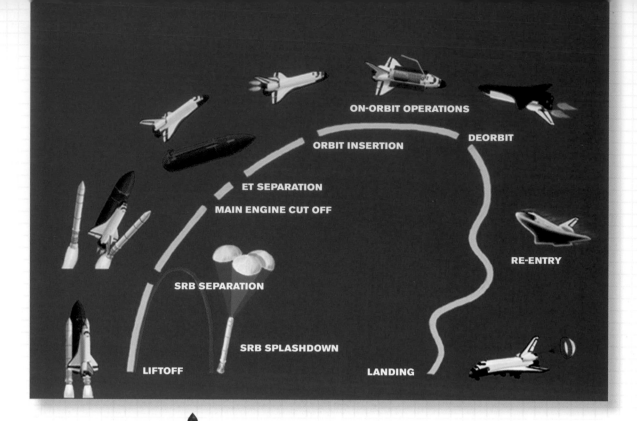

ON-ORBIT OPERATIONS

ORBIT INSERTION

DEORBIT

ET SEPARATION

MAIN ENGINE CUT OFF

RE-ENTRY

SRB SEPARATION

SRB SPLASHDOWN

LANDING

LIFTOFF

to keep the liquids inside cold. This insulation works amazingly well. If you put your hand on the foam, it feels only a little bit cool, even though the LOX inside is −297°F, and the LH_2 is −423°F. These super-cold liquids flow together and ignite at launch. The total thrust of a shuttle at liftoff, using both solid and liquid fuel, is 7 million pounds.

After the solid rocket boosters have used up all their propellant, they are jettisoned, or forced away from the orbiter, by exploding separation bolts. By then the shuttle is about 30 miles above Earth. As the solid rocket boosters fall away from the orbiter, one on each side, they begin their descent, first curving gracefully and then tumbling end over end until parachutes pop open to lower them safely into the Atlantic, where divers fish them out and return them to Kennedy Space Center, at Cape Canaveral, Florida. After thorough cleaning, they're sent back to the manufacturer in Utah, where they are refilled with solid rocket fuel and used again for later space flights.

As the flight continues the shuttle's main engines are fueled by LOX and LH_2 flowing through ducts from the ET at the rate of 62,000 gallons a minute. This creates a thrust of more than 1.2 million pounds to propel the orbiter into orbit at 17,500 miles per hour. This speed, called orbital velocity, is needed for the shuttle to reach and remain in low-Earth orbit. Then the ET is pushed away from the orbiter and somersaults very slowly into the atmosphere, where the heat of reentry burns off the foam that coats the outside of the tank. In spite of the ET's huge size, its aluminum skin beneath the foam insulation is only about an eighth of an inch thick. There will still be some LOX and LH_2 left in the ET. When the heat of reentry raises the pressure of this remaining propellant, the thin-skinned tank explodes. Its pieces rain down into the Indian Ocean, rarely to be seen again except by undersea creatures. That part of the shuttle is *not* reusable.

During the shuttle's first few years of operation, crews performed many demanding jobs. They made space-to-Earth observations for military services and launched communication satellites into orbit. On space walks they fixed satellites that needed repair. They experimented with the effects of zero gravity on people and plants and animals. Americans were still only mildly interested in the space program, but they became more enthusiastic in January 1984 when President Ronald Reagan announced, "We can follow our dreams to distant stars, living and working in space for peaceful economic and scientific gain. Tonight I am directing NASA to develop a permanently manned space station, and do it within a decade."

ɟɟWE CAN FOLLOW OUR DREAMS TO DISTANT STARS.ɟɟ

PRESIDENT REAGAN

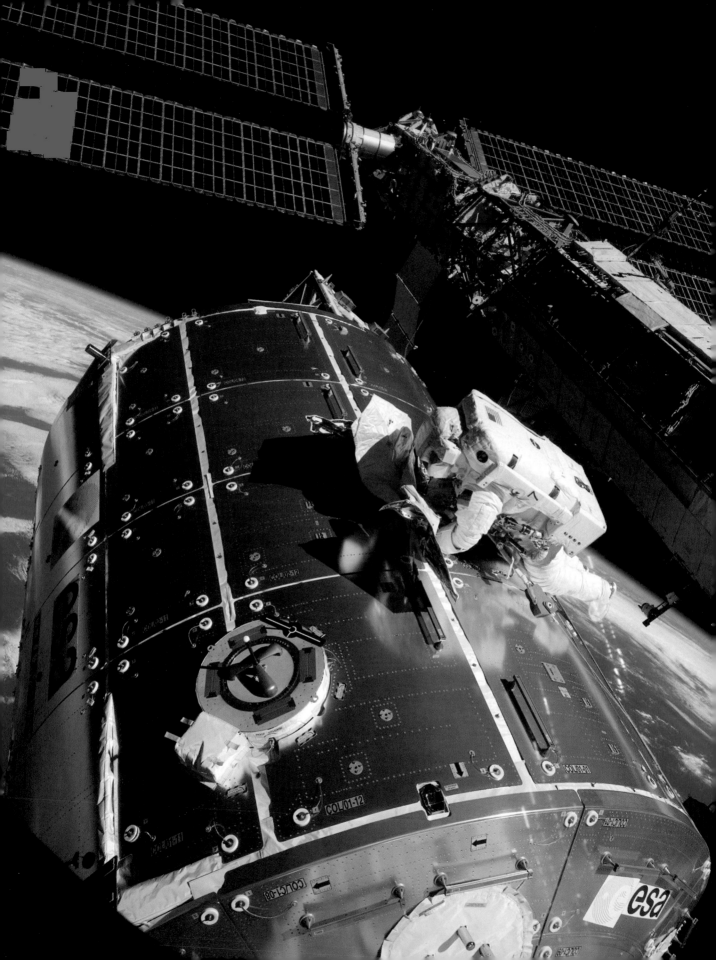

president Reagan's successors were quick to endorse his goals for the U.S. space program. In 1989 President George H. W. Bush announced that the space station would be a stepping-stone to putting bases on the Moon and Mars. Then in 1993, as the world eased into an era of international cooperation with the end of the Cold War, President Bill Clinton asked Russia to partner with the United States in building a permanently occupied space station. Although the U.S. and Russia were to be the main builders of the space station, Canada, Japan, Brazil, and the 13 member nations of the European Space Agency (Austria, Belgium, Denmark, France, Germany, Ireland, Italy, Netherlands, Norway, Spain, Sweden, Switzerland, and the United Kingdom) would also contribute parts and expertise.

Russia already had its Mir space station in orbit, and from 1995 to 1998, during the design phase of the International Space Station (ISS), seven U.S. astronauts lived on Russia's Mir with Russian cosmonauts for several months at a time. Russian cosmonauts flew on the U.S. space shuttle seven times, and nine space shuttle

DURING A SHUTTLE MISSION TO THE INTERNATIONAL SPACE STATION, ASTRONAUT REX WALHEIM INSTALLS HANDRAILS ON THE COLUMBUS LABORATORY.

missions docked with Mir to exchange crews and to deliver supplies.

In a series of firsts, the first ISS module (unit), named *Zarya*, was launched in November 1998 aboard a Russian Proton rocket, a liquid-fuel vehicle used only for unmanned cargo flights. A month later the U.S. shuttle *Endeavour* carried a module named *Unity* to join *Zarya*. The first full-time crew—one American astronaut and two Russian cosmonauts—reached the ISS in a Soyuz capsule in November 2000. A Soyuz also transported the first civilian space tourist, American Dennis Tito, in April 2001. To be accepted as a paying passenger (he never told how much he paid to spend six days in the ISS), Tito had to train in Moscow for six months before the flight.

From the end of 1998 to the end of 2002, 11 shuttle flights reached the ISS: five made by *Endeavour,* four by *Atlantis,* and two by *Discovery.* Each shuttle was capable of carrying a payload as big as a school bus to the space station. Three other trips were flown by Protons, single-use Russian spacecraft able to lift 21 tons of cargo.

Parts were installed by rotating crews of astronauts and cosmonauts who added framework, trusses, solar arrays, a robotic arm, a docking compartment, and an airlock. Piece by piece the ISS gradually took shape as the work space expanded, the scientific laboratories grew, and widening solar panels converted sunlight into electrical energy for operations.

Then tragedy struck the shuttle program. On February 1, 2003, the space shuttle *Columbia* broke up on its way back to Earth after one of its research missions. (None of *Columbia*'s 28 flights had ever been to the International Space Station. Most of its missions were to launch and repair space telescopes and communications satellites.) The loss of *Columbia* meant that every other shuttle flight had to be canceled until the cause of the tragedy was discovered and fixed.

Investigation results showed that on January 16, 2003, as *Columbia* and its crew blasted off from Kennedy Space Center, a chunk of insulating foam had broken away from its external fuel tank and had hit the edge of the shuttle's left wing. This would prove to be a fatal flaw on reentry.

THE CREW OF *COLUMBIA*'S 2003 MISSION, FROM LEFT TO RIGHT: DAVID M. BROWN, RICK D. HUSBAND, LAUREL B. CLARK, KALPANA CHAWLA, MICHAEL P. ANDERSON, WILLIAM C. MCCOOL, AND ILAN RAMON (A CITIZEN OF ISRAEL)

At the end of a mission, as a shuttle returns to Earth, it uses atmospheric drag as a brake to slow it down. In space flights "drag" is the term for the force that slows an object as it travels through the atmosphere. The thicker the atmosphere and the faster the object moves through it, the stronger the drag force becomes.

The atmosphere grows thinner as the distance from Earth's surface increases. For example, at an altitude of 250 miles, where the ISS orbits, there are only a few molecules of air in the atmosphere, but even those few small impacts are enough to slow the ISS down for a loss of about 328 feet in altitude each day. Controlled engine thrusts from visiting docked spacecraft "reboost" the ISS into the desired orbit. Closer to Earth, the air becomes "thicker." As a returning shuttle speeds through this ever thickening air, friction causes the temperature on its surface to grow hotter and hotter, rising all the way to 3000°F.

A shuttle's nose and wing edges are protected by four different kinds of heat-resistant materials, including the tiles you read about on page 45. Over a number of flights of the same shuttle, some heat-resistant tiles will break loose and peel away. As long as they don't all come off in the same area during a single flight, the vehicle will stay safe. Before the next flight each missing tile will be replaced, and each remaining tile will be minutely examined to make sure there's been no damage. Any damaged tiles will be replaced. At the time of the 2003 disaster more than 44 percent of *Columbia*'s heat tiles had been in place since they were glued there back in 1979. The rest were newer replacements.

The piece of insulating foam that flew off the external tank during launch knocked off several tiles, including a critical thermal tile on the wing's edge. Air that was superheated because of atmospheric drag blasted through that hole and melted aluminum within the wing structure. The wing failed, *Columbia* broke apart, and seven astronauts died.

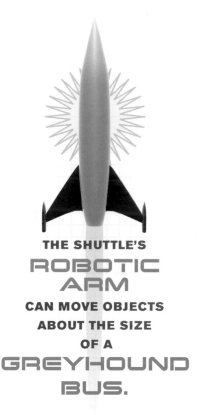

THE SHUTTLE'S
ROBOTIC
ARM
CAN MOVE OBJECTS
ABOUT THE SIZE
OF A
GREYHOUND
BUS.

THE EUROPEAN SPACE
AGENCY BUILT THE
COLUMBUS LABORATORY.
IT WAS TRANSPORTED TO
THE ISS ABOARD THE SPACE
SHUTTLE *ATLANTIS.*

Columbia was the second shuttle destroyed in an accident. In 1986 the shuttle *Challenger* had exploded very soon after takeoff, also with a loss of seven astronauts. One of them, Christa McAuliffe, was on her way to becoming the first teacher in space. *Challenger*'s failure was caused by weather conditions. Low temperatures during takeoff kept a part from sealing the way it was supposed to.

Why do these accidents happen? Aren't rocket scientists careful enough? They try to be, and they take their responsibilities extremely seriously, as do all the workers in the space program. But each space shuttle has more than 2.5 million parts, including 230 miles of wire, 1,060 valves, 1,440 circuit breakers, and hundreds of other components. With numbers like these, it's inevitable that parts will sometimes fail. And the shuttles are growing old.

For two and a half years after the loss of *Columbia* all shuttle flights were canceled as experts studied

YURI MALENCHENKO

PEGGY WHITSON

YI SO-YEON

ways to improve shuttle safety. But astronauts were still working up there in the International Space Station, and they had to be brought home. New crews had to be ferried to the ISS to continue assembling the station and to add the big laboratories and experiments and supplies that were being produced by Japan and the European Space Agency as well as by the United States and Russia. Russia's *Soyuz* was the only spacecraft that could carry supplies and crew members to the ISS and back while the shuttles were grounded.

Coming back to Earth in a *Soyuz* crew capsule can sometimes turn into a rocky ride. Though shuttle flights had been restored, in April 2008 three space travelers climbed aboard a *Soyuz* capsule for a return trip from the ISS to Russia. Russian flight engineer Yuri Malenchenko had spent six months on the ISS performing experiments. Peggy A. Whitson of NASA, the first female astronaut ever to command a space station, had just set a new American record—a total of 377 days—for the most time spent in orbit aboard the ISS. The third passenger was Yi So-yeon, a 29-year-old bioengineering student from South Korea.

A *Soyuz* reentry is very different from a shuttle reentry. First, the *Soyuz* moves out from its docking port on the space station, backing away at about four inches per second. When it's 12 miles from the ISS, the engines fire to slow down the spacecraft for reentry. The descent module, which holds the crew, continues plummeting toward Earth, protected by its heat shield from the friction caused by atmospheric drag. A parachute opens to slow the final descent of the capsule to the ground.

In that 2008 return flight a heat shield slipped, and the crew capsule encountered the atmosphere at

a steep angle, causing the three astronauts to feel gravitational forces of more than 8 g's—eight times more gravity than we feel on Earth. This slammed them back against their seats and exerted great pressure on their lungs, making it hard for them to breathe. The inside of the capsule got so hot from atmospheric drag that So-yeon feared it would catch on fire.

THIS ART SHOWS THE STEEP ANGLE OF A BALLISTIC REENTRY. DURING THE APRIL 2008 DESCENT THE *SOYUZ* CREW EXPERIENCED A GRAVITATIONAL PULL EIGHT TIMES STRONGER THAN THAT ON EARTH.

Despite the slowing action of its parachute, the *Soyuz* hit the ground hard, bouncing onto and scorching a field in northern Kazakhstan, 260 miles from where it should have landed. A helicopter search team that was sent to pick up the astronauts didn't know where they were. After Malenchenko crawled out of the capsule, some local herdsmen helped Whitson and So-yeon to lie down outside in the shadow of the landed spacecraft. Luckily, all three lived to tell what had happened.

A NASA report written after the *Columbia* accident stated that "rockets still fail between 2 and 5 percent of the time. This is true of just about any launch vehicle—Atlas, Delta, Soyuz, Shuttle—regardless of what nation builds it or what basic configuration is used; they all fail about the same amount of the time. Building and launching rockets is still a very dangerous business, and will continue to be so for the foreseeable future while we gain experience at it."

So is it worth it? Absolutely! The best way to explore and learn about the universe is to leave Earth behind.

"BUILDING AND LAUNCHING ROCKETS IS STILL A VERY DANGEROUS BUSINESS."

NASA REPORT

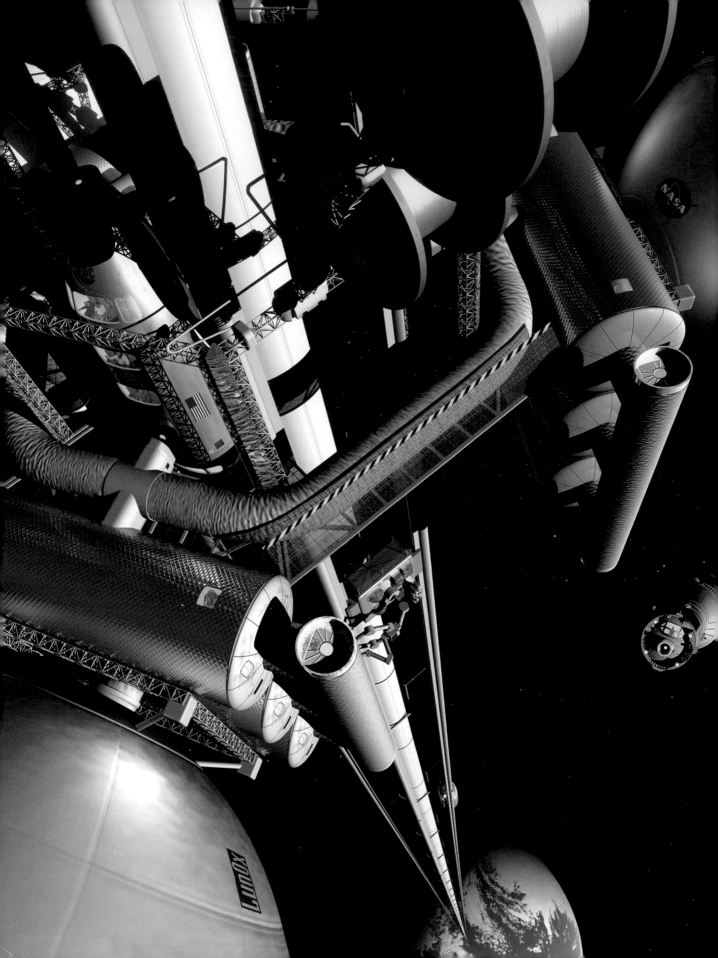

Elon Musk knows what success feels like, but he has lived through failure more than once. Musk was born in South Africa. At the age of 18 he came alone to the United States to attend the University of Pennsylvania, where he received double degrees in economics and physics. He recalls, "When I was in college, I thought there were three areas that would most affect the future of humanity." His three forecasts were the Internet, clean energy, and space exploration.

He started with Internet online services, designing a method of money transfer that evolved into PayPal. He sold that service for a lot of money. By the age of 28 Musk had earned a fortune worth hundreds of millions of dollars. In 2001 he began to think about space exploration, especially about a way to send humans to Mars, another of those three areas he believed would affect the future of humanity. He wanted to "make humanity a multi-planet species."

A SPACE ELEVATOR COULD LIFT CARGO FROM EARTH THROUGH THOUSANDS OF MILES OF OUTER SPACE. THE TECHNOLOGY IS STILL FAR IN THE FUTURE, BUT IT MAY HAPPEN ONE DAY.

Bringing together a group of highly talented engineers experienced in building everything from high-performance sailboats to rocket engines, Musk founded Space

Exploration Technologies (SpaceX). His timing was good. In 2004 President George W. Bush declared, "Returning to the Moon is an important step for our space program....With the experience and knowledge gained on the Moon, we will then be ready to take the next steps of space exploration: human missions to Mars and to worlds beyond."

Why are space dreamers so eager to reach Mars? It may have begun back in the 1890s when American astronomer Percival Lowell observed Mars through his telescope in Arizona and believed he saw canals. Not the kind eroded by nature, but waterways built by live beings.

Science-fiction writers added to the excitement with novels like Ray Bradbury's *The Martian Chronicles*. Clear telescope images, photos from planetary flybys, and soil

THE CONSTELLATION PROGRAM TO RETURN TO THE MOON WOULD USE DIFFERENT VEHICLES FOR TAKEOFF, ORBITING, LANDING, TRAVEL ON THE MOON'S SURFACE, AND LIFTOFF FOR RETURNING TO EARTH.

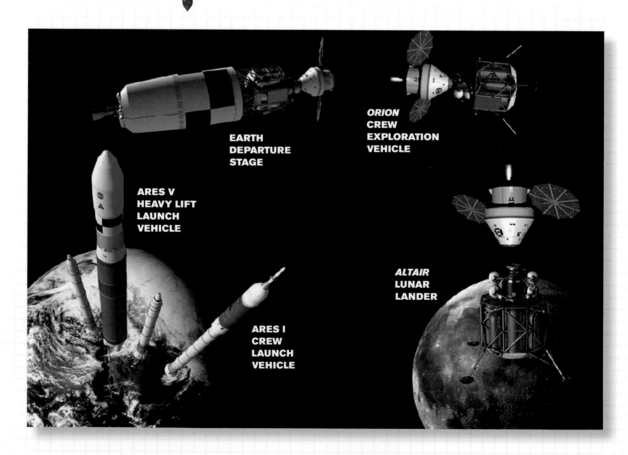

EARTH DEPARTURE STAGE

ORION CREW EXPLORATION VEHICLE

ARES V HEAVY LIFT LAUNCH VEHICLE

ARES I CREW LAUNCH VEHICLE

ALTAIR LUNAR LANDER

THE SHORTEST
DISTANCE FROM
EARTH
TO
MARS
WILL BE ABOUT
35 MILLION
MILES!

sampling by robots landing on Mars's barren surface have convinced most Earthlings that if there is any life on Mars, it's microscopic. Still, the fascination remains, and the goal persists. People want to go there.

But the Moon has to come first—again. Constellation is the name of the program being studied to return Americans to the Moon. NASA is developing two new launch vehicles, Ares I (one) and Ares V (five) as part of the Constellation program, proposed to be built between 2010 and 2016. Ares I is made up of a five-segment shuttle solid-fuel booster with a hydrogen-fueled upper stage, more advanced but pretty much the same technology as in the Apollo days. A much more powerful, unmanned rocket called the Ares V is being developed to launch lunar landers.

During the Apollo Moon missions, astronauts flew from Earth to the Moon inside a cone-shaped capsule. If all goes as planned, four as-yet-unnamed astronauts will fly inside the cone-shaped *Orion* capsule now being designed to travel from Earth to the Moon. Orion? Surprisingly, NASA has revived the name of the nuclear-rocket proposal from the 1960s.

It's hoped that space travelers will be able to use the Moon as a takeoff point for a trip to Mars. Mark Geyer, manager of the new Orion project, believes that if we want to go to Mars, we first need to practice living on the Moon, building quarters there, and learning to move in gravity that's one-sixth as strong as Earth's. But NASA expert Howard McCurdy cautions that the Moon "will become its own destination, for hundreds of years. The easy way to go to the Moon is the hard way to go to Mars."

The space shuttles are an aging fleet with problems worrisome enough to delay launches. By March 2009 a

 ELON MUSK (TAN SHIRT) AND THE SPACEX LAUNCH TEAM WATCH FROM MISSION CONTROL AS THE FALCON 1 ROCKET LIFTS OFF FROM OMELEK ISLAND IN THE PACIFIC OCEAN.

a *Discovery* flight to the ISS had been postponed four times because of concerns about cracks in a valve coming from the fuel tank. Because of problems that could become dangerous as well as costly, NASA may retire the shuttles at the end of 2010. Between the shuttles' retirement and the debut of Ares I and *Orion,* NASA astronauts will be forced to hitch rides in *Soyuz* capsules launched on Soyuz rockets to and from the ISS. Or maybe not. That's where Elon Musk comes into the picture.

If all goes well, Musk's SpaceX company will be the new taxi service to the ISS. SpaceX developed its first rocket, a two-stage launch vehicle powered by LOX and kerosene. Named Falcon 1, the rocket stands 70 feet tall and lifts off with a thrust of 78,000 pounds. The first Falcon 1 was test-fired from the SpaceX launch site on Omelek Island in the Marshall Islands in the Pacific. It failed when the first-stage engine shut down less than a minute after liftoff due to a broken fuel line. When the rocket crashed back to Earth, the satellite payload flew off the booster and landed on the island, battered but not destroyed.

Failure hurts. No matter how rich or smart you are, no matter how many people are rooting for you, it hurts to fail. *Wired* magazine described the reaction of Musk and his team after the failure: "Overhead sparkled [the constellation] Orion, and low on the horizon, the Southern Cross. Musk was somber. A few guys were crying. Four years of seven-day workweeks and tens of millions of dollars: blown.

Finally Musk spoke: 'When we started, we all knew we could fail on the first mission,' he said. 'But we will build another rocket and try again.'"

And that's what they did. On the fourth try Falcon 1 achieved orbit—the first successful flight of a privately funded, liquid-fuel rocket. Musk shouted, "That was frickin' awesome! There's only a handful of countries on Earth that have done this. It's usually a country thing, not a company thing. We did it! Definitely one of the best days of my life."

All the other space programs on Earth have been established and developed by national governments. After its Falcon 1 success, SpaceX did receive a 1.6-billion-dollar NASA contract to deliver cargo to the ISS. Falcon continues to fly, and the new, larger, and stronger Falcon 9 rocket can deliver large satellites or SpaceX's reusable *Dragon* spacecraft to orbit. The plan is to have Falcon 9 and *Dragon* transport passengers, freeing NASA to use *Orion* for flights to and from the Moon. Since delays in developing *Orion* and Ares continue, Musk says his craft are "the only chance that NASA has of having astronaut transport after the shuttle retirement." Without them to reduce the gap between the time the shuttle retires and *Orion* starts flying, "We'll be thumbing rides from the Russians for another five or six years. And paying a lot."

The first Falcon 9/*Dragon* flights will carry only cargo, but NASA can ask SpaceX to demonstrate a crew-carrying *Dragon* mission for as many as seven astronauts. Musk says, "I want to make rockets a hundred times, if not a thousand times better. Thirty years from now, there'll be a base on the moon and on Mars, and people will be going back and forth on SpaceX rockets."

Rocket scientists are working on new technical marvels to move cargo and people farther into outer space. One project is called the Space Elevator, but Musk remarks, "It will be a long time, if ever, before the economics of a space elevator make sense."

A group of engineers at Cambridge University in England totally disagrees with Musk's statement. Arthur C. Clarke, a scientist as well as a science-fiction writer, once caught the attention of space fans in his novel *The Fountains of Paradise* by writing, "If the laws of celestial mechanics make it possible for an object to stay fixed in the sky, might it not be possible to lower a cable down to the surface and so establish an elevator system linking Earth to space?" Clarke imagined an elevator that could climb into outer space bearing cargo and passengers. But even before he wrote that idea, it had been proposed by none other than Konstantin

> **"WE'LL BE THUMBING RIDES FROM THE RUSSIANS FOR ANOTHER FIVE OR SIX YEARS."**
>
> ELON MUSK

Tsiolkovsky, who in 1895 came up with the same thought when he saw the Eiffel Tower in Paris.

So what is a space elevator? This is how it would work. A spacecraft would go into orbit at 22,000 miles above Earth. That's the altitude at which telecommunications satellites orbit as they remain in the same orbital position with regard to a site on Earth. You could draw a straight line from the satellite to a point at the Equator and the line wouldn't change direction. This is called a geosynchronous or geostationary orbit. (Clarke is the person who proposed a geosynchronous orbit, and now it's real.) From that altitude a geosynchronous satellite completes one orbit around Earth in the same amount of time that Earth makes one rotation on its axis. This is why the satellite remains in that exact same position in relation to a particular point on Earth's surface. From these high orbits, communications satellites send telephone and television signals to your house.

To build a space elevator, a rocket would first have to lift into orbit a spool containing a tether—or you can call it a ribbon or a cable—that's wound around the spool. Once in Earth orbit, the spool would begin to unwind, dropping the bottom of the tether back to Earth where it would be anchored to a platform in the ocean near the Equator. In space, the spool would keep moving to orbits higher and higher until it reached an altitude of 62,000 miles, all the while unwinding the tether. (The average orbital altitude of the ISS is only 250 miles.) At the top of the tether would be a counterweight that would orbit Earth and keep the tether taut, just as a ball at the end of a string keeps the string tight and straight when you whirl the ball over your head. Earth's rotation would keep the counterweight circling outward,

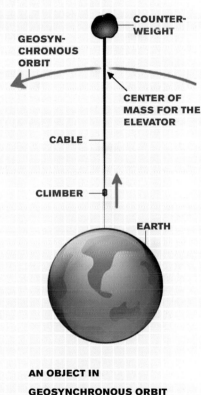

AN OBJECT IN GEOSYNCHRONOUS ORBIT MUST REMAIN PRECISELY ABOVE ITS POSITIONING POINT ON THE EQUATOR. THE COUNTERWEIGHT IN A SPACE ELEVATOR WOULD HOLD THE CABLE TAUT.

high and fast—but always directly above the anchor platform.

The platform that would lift cargo and passengers is called a climber. To boost a climber, three power sources are possible: nuclear energy, solar power, and laser power. The best method would probably be laser power beamed up from the anchor platform with an extra assist from solar power from above. The underside of the climber would be lined with what are called photovoltaic arrays. Laser light focusing on these arrays would boost the climber at a speed not much greater than 120 miles per hour. That's hardly faster than your car can go. It would take more than a week for people to ride up 22,000 miles in the space elevator, but that's not the big problem. The worry is that they'd pass through a belt of heavy radiation for several days. This would not be good for people, but it wouldn't be too damaging to cargo. The advantage would be cost—about $100 to $400 per pound, compared to the $2,000 to $60,000 per pound it costs today to launch cargo aboard a rocket. That's quite a savings!

But there's another possibility. Scientists have known for some years that if two bodies are rotating at opposite ends of a tether, they will fly off into different orbits if the tether is broken. To understand how this would work, think of two ice-skaters holding hands as one spins the other in a circle on the ice. When they let go of each other, the one who was being spun shoots across the ice at high speed. Skaters call this fun maneuver "crack the whip," and it could be a way to fling crews and cargo from the top of the space tether all the way to Mars. The payload's trajectory would have to be tightly controlled, which is just one of countless problems with the whole space elevator concept.

The tether is the main challenge. It needs to be three feet wide, thinner than a newspaper page, and hundreds of times stronger than steel but only one-fifth steel's weight. There was no known material on Earth that could fit those requirements until, in 1991, scientists discovered carbon nanotubes. These hollow carbon tubes are 100 times stronger than steel. They're so tiny that 50,000 of them would fit inside a human hair. (The prefix "nano" means "one billionth," so one nanometer is one-billionth of a meter wide.) They're the strongest material known to science, and at six times lighter than steel they fill the weight requirement for a space-elevator tether. Until now, nanotubes could only be woven into sections a couple of inches long. But English scientists from Cambridge University have found a way to combine nanotubes into longer strands. Describing their nanotubes' structure, one researcher says, "[T]hey entangle and hold hands." Though he admits that the creation of strong enough material still might take five to ten more years, he adds, "You have to aim high."

Rocket science always aims high.

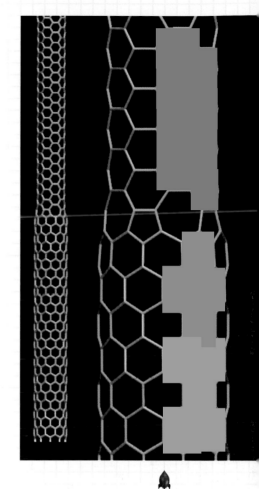

NANOTUBES ARE MICROSCOPIC, BUT THEY CAN BE WOVEN INTO MATERIAL THAT'S EXTREMELY STRONG AND LIGHTWEIGHT.

The universe is vast. The speed of light is fast. (Science-fiction writers have always imagined astronauts traveling at the speed of light or at warp speed, which is entirely different.) Is either of these possible? Certainly not now and probably not ever.

The fastest objects flying toward the planets aren't carrying humans; they are spacecraft carrying scientific instruments to study the universe. Some land, like the robots on Mars and the European Space Agency's *Rosetta*, which is scheduled to deliver a lander to a comet in 2014. Others keep traveling deeper into space, sending back data. The *New Horizons* probe races toward Pluto at speeds as fast as 51,449 miles an hour in a 9-year journey that will take it more than 4 billion miles from Earth, where light from the Sun will be a thousand times dimmer than here on Earth.

At that distance sunlight would be too weak to propel a solar sail. What are solar sails? They're another science-fiction favorite. In *Star Wars: Episode II—Attack of the Clones* Count Dooku escapes in a solar-sail-propelled

LASER POWER STATIONS MIGHT ONE DAY PROPEL SPACECRAFT THROUGHOUT THE SOLAR SYSTEM, AS IN THIS ARTIST'S CONCEPT.

THE IDEA
OF USING
SOLAR
SAILS
FOR SPACE TRAVEL
CAN BE
TRACED TO
17TH-CENTURY
ASTRONOMER
JOHANNES KEPLER.

spacecraft, one that wouldn't work very well in real space because in the movie its sails are shaped wrong.

In 1964 Arthur C. Clarke wrote this in a short story:

Hold your hands out to the sun. What do you feel? Heat, of course. But there's pressure as well—though you've never noticed it, because it's so tiny. Over the area of your hands, it only comes to about a millionth of an ounce. But out in space, even a pressure as small as that can be important—for it's acting all the time, hour after hour, day after day. Unlike rocket fuel, it's free and unlimited.

Clarke was describing solar sails—giant, flat sheets of a material that's 40 to 100 times thinner than a piece of writing paper. The sheets' mirrorlike surfaces reflect light particles from the Sun. The pressure of these particles, known as photons, is very slight, yet it exerts a constant force, pushing solar sails to speeds of several hundred thousand miles per hour when the sail faces the Sun. Just as with a sail on a boat, a solar sail can be angled so the photon pressure will move it in the desired direction. Because they need no other propellant, solar sails should be able to keep accelerating as long as photons keep hitting them.

This has actually been attempted. After a lot of planning and experimentation, the first solar sail, named *Cosmos 1*, took off in 2005 on top of a Volna rocket that was launched from a Russian submarine. The rocket reached 45 miles into space but then fell back into the ocean, with the solar sail still on board. The sail was never found.

NanoSail-D was NASA's original solar sail project. According to Edward "Sandy" Montgomery of NASA's Marshall Space Flight Center, "The structure is made of aluminum and space-age plastic. The whole spacecraft

MATERIALS SCIENTISTS HAVE CREATED AN AMAZINGLY LIGHTWEIGHT MATERIAL TO FORM SOLAR SAILS, WHICH REFLECT LIGHT PARTICLES FROM THE SUN.

weighs less than ten pounds." Fully expanded in the laboratory before it was folded and packed for launch, the kite-shaped sail spread out to about 100 square feet of thin, light-catching material. Sandy adds, "It's not so much about how far a sail will go compared to a rocket; the key is *how fast*."

NanoSail-D took off on Elon Musk's third Falcon 1 launch attempt, which lasted just two minutes. Like *Cosmos 1*, *NanoSail-D* ended up in the ocean, although the two vanished solar-sail cargoes were literally oceans apart. Failure happens.

Success happens, too. The *Dawn* spacecraft took off right at dawn on a Delta II rocket that had nine solid fuel boosters. A million pounds of thrust lifted *Dawn* off the Cape Canaveral launchpad, sending it on its way to Mars and even farther, toward the asteroid Vesta and the dwarf planet Ceres. *Dawn* is driven by ion propulsion, another recent technology with roots that reach back decades. Way back in 1906 Robert Goddard suggested a system that would use electric fields to accelerate charged ions at high velocities. In the 1950s von Braun wrote, "The small thrust is effective for missions to the more distant parts of the solar system." And that's where *Dawn* is heading.

Ion propulsion is a great way to move spacecraft through space, but the spacecraft has to lift off with a much stronger launch force than ion propulsion can provide. That's why a Delta II rocket gave *Dawn* its boost off the launchpad. Sixty-two minutes after launch, *Dawn* broke free of the Delta II and unfurled giant solar wings that stretch 65 feet from edge to edge. The solar wings provide power to an ion thruster aboard the spacecraft.

Chemical rockets must use very large amounts of propellant to lift their payloads. The fuel needed to get the space shuttle into orbit weighs 20 times more than the shuttle itself. That's why launches cost so much. Ion engines take very small amounts of fuel and expel it at much higher speeds, but only *after* they reach outer space. Because of the low rate of fuel consumption, ion propulsion isn't strong enough to get a ship off the launchpad and into space. A space probe's speed must reach about 25,000 miles per hour to escape Earth's gravity and continue on its voyage. But once it gets up there, an ion spacecraft uses a lot less fuel and keeps building up speed, going faster and faster.

Dawn reached space carrying less than a thousand pounds of a gas called xenon. A NASA Web site explains, "Unlike chemical engines, which can be operated for minutes, or in extreme cases, for an hour or so, ion engines can be operated for years. The effect of the gentle thrust slowly builds up, eventually attaining speeds far beyond the reach of conventional propellants." *Dawn* will travel three billion miles over eight years.

An ion is a charged particle consisting of an atom that has either lost or gained electrons. Each xenon atom consists of a tiny, dense nucleus surrounded by a cloud

"ION ENGINES CAN BE OPERATED FOR YEARS."
NASA REPORT

of 54 electrons. Inside *Dawn's* ion thruster, an electron beam bombards the xenon atoms. When this beam knocks an electron out of an atom, the result is an electrically unbalanced atom: 54 positive charges against 53 negative charges. High voltage shoots these ions through a metal grid at very high velocities to propel *Dawn.* The thrust produced is very small, but over time the constant slight push can achieve very high speeds. Speed keeps building as the mission continues. A year and a half after launch, *Dawn* had already flown more than 621 million miles and had passed Mars, but its planned trip to Vesta and Ceres won't be completed until 2015. For not quite a thousand pounds of propellant that's very good mileage—a lot of bang for the buck. Without ion propulsion, NASA couldn't afford *Dawn.*

Marc Rayman, *Dawn's* chief engineer, says, "[*Dawn*] communicates with us, follows our instructions, and returns information, but it is on its own as it journeys to explore distant, alien worlds. It will return pictures and other scientific information on worlds so remote that humans have just barely glimpsed them even with the most powerful telescopes. I love thinking about

A MILLION POUNDS OF THRUST FROM A DELTA II ROCKET LIFTED *DAWN* FROM THE LAUNCHPAD ON SEPTEMBER 27, 2007.

that spacecraft as it crosses millions and millions and millions of miles of interplanetary space, carrying with it my hopes and dreams and my longing to continue the journeys my mind began as I looked up at the night sky in my backyard when I was a child."

Dr. Rayman adds, "Everyone who cares about science, everyone who shares in the quest for knowledge, everyone who has the passion for understanding more about our place in the universe, everyone who wonders what really is 'out there' owns this spacecraft."

But what about humans who want to climb aboard spaceships and travel past Mars to fly even farther into the solar system? Will it ever be possible? Yes!

Everything depends on the intelligence, the

DAWN WILL TRAVEL BEYOND MARS TO STUDY THE ASTEROID VESTA AND THE DWARF PLANET CERES. FAR-FLYING SPACECRAFT BUILD OUR KNOWLEDGE OF OUR SOLAR SYSTEM AND BEYOND.

imagination, the dedication, and the endless hours of effort put in by engineers, mathematicians, scientists, astronomers, information technologists—and of course the people who build everything and test it. Many new technologies are now in various stages of design. One of them, which has already reached the test stage, is called magneto-plasma propulsion. The project's full name is Variable Specific Impulse Magnetoplasma Rocket (VASIMR for short).

The two parts to that term are "magneto" and "plasma." "Plasma" means "very hot gas." Plasma can reach temperatures close to those of the Sun. You see it in lightning, in very hot flames, in the auroras, and in the stars. Plasma's energy is so great that it vaporizes any material it touches.

How can scientists work with these gaseous substances when they're heated to tens of thousands of degrees? Plasma is a partially ionized gas, in which some of its electrons are not bound to an atom or molecule particles. In VASIMR natural gas is fed into a chamber where high power radio waves convert it into plasma. The mixture can be controlled and guided by strong magnetic fields—the "magneto" part of the term.

The magnets in the engine line up the plasma particles that are moving at tremendous speeds to shoot them out and create thrust. The magnetic fields also keep any nearby substances, such as rocket surfaces, from melting in the extreme heat. With rockets, the higher the temperature of the gases inside the core, the faster they propel the exhaust— and plasma rockets will be hundreds of times more propellant-efficient than chemical rockets.

PLASMA MAKES UP 99 PERCENT OF THE VISIBLE UNIVERSE.

Dr. Franklin Chang Diaz heads the Ad Astra Rocket Company. He's not only a plasma physicist, but also a former astronaut and a veteran of seven space shuttle flights. Speaking about VASIMR, he says, "With this technology we could get to Mars as fast as 39 days. This soup of charged particles is not unlike the Sun and the stars, and the hotter the exhaust, the better the rocket." He explains that, as with *Dawn,* a traditional chemical rocket would first lift the spaceship into orbit, and "then from orbit we would move on with plasma drive, like the starship *Enterprise.* We would use it for transportation from one planet to another."

As a young boy Chang Diaz wrote to Wernher von Braun asking how he could become an astronaut. Responding by letter, von Braun advised Franklin to get a scientific or engineering degree. Chang Diaz took this advice and received his doctoral degree in applied plasma physics from the Massachusetts Institute of Technology (MIT). Recently, 12 students in MIT's Department of Aeronautics and Astronautics created a miniature version of VASIMR by making their own small rocket out of an empty Coke can and a plastic water bottle. They built it for fun, but the magneto-plasma rocket science was real—and it worked! This is how exciting future technologies are born.

And yet, envisioning missions to Mars and the farther planets, Dr. Chang Diaz predicts, "Future human interplanetary spacecraft will rely on nuclear power to explore the far reaches of the solar system and beyond."

Nuclear power? As in the Project Orion ideas of Stan Ulam and Theodore Taylor and Freeman Dyson?

"WITH THIS TECHNOLOGY WE COULD GET TO MARS AS FAST AS 39 DAYS."

DR. FRANKLIN CHANG DIAZ

The saying "what goes around comes around" seems appropriate when applied to rocket science. Nuclear spacecraft have actually orbited Earth for many years. Russia has launched more than 30 nuclear-fission reactors in space vehicles. The United States has flown only one, in 1965, but more may be coming.

Nuclear space vehicles wouldn't be used to orbit Earth. Instead, they would transport human travelers vast distances through outer space. How soon? Stan Ulam believed "the revolutions which are taking place happen more frequently and proceed faster than all the wise prophesies would let us anticipate...." And Freeman Dyson said, "I'm strongly interested in spreading life...enlarging the human domain of life. It's hardly begun adapting itself to the universe."

Are you ready to travel into space? The universe is waiting for you!

VASIMR MAY ONE DAY CARRY HUMANS TO MARS AND EVEN FARTHER. FLYING FASTER MEANS WE CAN TRAVEL FARTHER.

GLOSSARY

AERODYNAMICS
the motion of air and other gases reacting on objects

ATMOSPHERE
the envelope of air surrounding Earth; also the body of gases surrounding any planet or celestial body

ATMOSPHERIC DRAG
the resistance air or gas molecules exert on a body moving through them. Drag causes friction and creates heat.

BOOSTER ROCKET
the first stage of a rocket that has more than one stage

ENGINE
in spacecraft, a rocket or thruster that burns propellants

EXHAUST
gaseous or other particles flowing from the nozzle of a rocket while propellant burns

FORCE
a push or pull acting against an object that has mass. Force can cause the object to move or to change direction.

FUEL
a substance that when combined with an oxidizer burns to produce thrust in a rocket

LAUNCH
the lifting of a space vehicle from the ground by the force of thrust from its engines

MASS
the quantity of matter in a body. The mass of a body remains the same everywhere, but the body's weight changes according to the force of gravity acting upon it.

MILLISECOND
one-thousandth of a second

MISSILE
an object or a weapon that is propelled toward a target

NOZZLE
the rear opening of a rocket engine through which exhaust gases push to produce thrust

NUCLEAR FISSION
the splitting of the nucleus of an atom to release energy

ORBIT
the path that a body in space takes around another body in space

OXIDIZER
a substance necessary for the combustion of any fuel or propellant

PHOTOVOLTAIC CELLS
paper-thin solar cells that convert sunlight into electricity

PLASMA
a high-energy gas that responds to both electricity and magnetism

PROBE
an unmanned vehicle carrying instruments to gather information in space

PROPELLANT
a combination of oxidizer and fuel that burns to produce thrust in a rocket

PROPULSION
the method that drives an object's motion

RADIATION BELT
a layer of high-energy particles trapped by the magnetic field around Earth; also called the Van Allen belt.

RADIOACTIVE FALLOUT
particles that fall to Earth as a result of a nuclear explosion

REENTRY
a vehicle's descent into Earth's atmosphere from space

ROCKET
a missile or vehicle propelled by burning oxidized fuel

SATELLITE
any object, natural or manufactured, that orbits around a larger body. The term usually describes moons and unmanned spacecraft.

SOLAR ARRAY
a sheet of light-sensitive cells that gather photons from the Sun to generate electricity; also called a solar panel

SOLAR WIND
streams of plasma flowing from the Sun

SPACE
the universe beyond Earth's atmosphere, a boundary usually defined as beginning about 100 miles above Earth's surface

THRUST
the force, usually measured in pounds, produced by a rocket motor ejecting gases at high velocity through a nozzle

VACUUM
empty space

WARP SPEED
an unreal concept from *Star Trek*

BOOKS

Anderson, John D. Jr. *Introduction to Flight*. NY: McGraw Hill, 2007.

Brzezinski, Matthew. *Red Moon Rising: Sputnik and the Hidden Rivalries That Ignited the Space Age*. NY: Times Books, Henry Holt and Company, 2007.

Clarke, Arthur C. *The Fountains of Paradise*. London: Victor Gollancz Ltd., 1979.

Clarke, Arthur C. *"Sunjammer"* from *The Collected Stories of Arthur C. Clarke*. London: Victor Gollancz Ltd., 2001.

Darling, David. *The Complete Book of Spaceflight, From Apollo to Zero Gravity*. Hoboken, NJ: John Wiley & Sons, Inc., 2003.

Dewar, James A: *To the End of the Solar System: The Story of the Nuclear Rocket*. Burlington, Ontario, Canada: Collector's Guide Publishing, Inc., 2008.

Dyson, George: *Project Orion: The True Story of the Atomic Spaceship*. NY: Holt Paperbacks, 2003.

Kosmodemyanksky, A. *Konstantin Tsiolkovsky: His Life and Work*. Stockton, CA: University Press of the Pacific, 2000.

McDougall, Walter A: *The Heavens and the Earth: A Political History of the Space Age*. NY: Basic Books, 1985.

Skurzynski, Gloria: *Are We Alone? Scientists Search for Life in Space*. National Geographic Society, Washington, DC: 2004.

Stuckey, Mary E. *Slipping the Surly Bonds: Reagan's* Challenger *Address*. College Station, TX: Texas A&M University Press, 2006.

Ulam, Stanislaw M. *Adventures of a Mathematician*. Berkeley, CA: University of California Press, 1991.

von Braun, Wernher. *Project MARS: A Technical Tale*. Burlington, Ontario, Canada: Collector's Guide Publishing, Inc., 2006.

von Braun, Wernher and Frederick I. Ordway, III. *History of Rocketry & Space Travel,* revised edition. NY: Thomas Y. Crowell Company, 1969.

WEB SITES

Ad Astra: www.adastrarocket.com/home1.html

Challenger Center for Space Science Education: www.challenger.org

Jet Propulsion Laboratory: www.jpl.nasa.gov/

NASA Education: www.nasa.gov/offices/education/about/index.html

NASA For Students: www.nasa.gov/audience/forstudents/index.html

NASA Kids: http://kids.msfc.nasa.gov

NASA Quest: http://quest.nasa.gov

Science@NASA: http://science.msfc.nasa.gov

Spacekids: www.spacekids.com

The Space Place: http://spaceplace.jpl.nasa.gov/spacepl.htm

SpaceX: www.spacex.com/

QUOTE SOURCES

Note: For complete bibliographic information see authors and titles listed under Books.

P. 9 "When it was lit..." Anderson, p.703; pp. 11–12 Newton's laws see http://www.grc.nasa.gov/WWW/K-12/airplane/newton.html; p. 15 Tsiolkovsky: "For a long time..." Kosmodemyanksky, p.37; p. 16 Tsiolkovsky: "Earth is the...*National Geographic*, November 1988, p. 612; "[v]isualize...an elongated metal chamber..." From a letter written in 1911. ICEUM4, 10-15 July 2000, ESTEC, Noordwijk, The Netherlands Gulnara Omarova, National Aerospace Agency, http://conferences.esa.int/Moon2000/index.html ; Tsiolkovsky: "The chamber is partly occupied by a large store of substances..." http://engforum.pravda.ru/archive/index.php/t-87187.html; p. 17 Goddard: "I imagined how wonderful it would be..." *Propulsion Techniques: Action and Reaction* (Library of Flight Series), Peter J. Turchi, editor, American Institute of Aeronautics & Astronautics, Reston, VA: 1998; p. 18 "That Professor Goddard..." *New York Times*, January 13, 1920, p. 12, p. 19 Oberth: "rockets...so [powerful]..." *Die Rackete su den Planetenraumen*, Hermann Oberth, R. Oldenburg, Munich, 1923; p. 21 "Twenty-five seconds had elapsed..." "At an altitude of seventeen miles..." Brzezinski, pp. 2, 3; p. 22 "subversion in a new field..." *Korolev: How One Man Masterminded the Soviet Drive to Beat America to the Moon,* James Harford, Wiley, Hoboken, NJ, 1999, p. 49; p. 23 Korolev: "The purpose of this rocket is to get there!..." "Sergei Pavlovich Korolev: The Soviet Space Program's Secret Mastermind" Gareth Branwyn. http://www.streettech.com/modules.php?op=modload&name=News&file=article&sid=1616; von Braun: "My name is Magnus von Braun..." McDougall, p. 44; p. 27 Chertok: "We regarded it as Korolev's little toy!..." BBC News: "Sputnik engineer's memories Oct 3, 2007," http://news.bbc.co.uk/player/nol/newsid_7020000/newsid_7026900/7026984.stm?bw=bb&mp=wm&asb=1&news=1&bbcws=1; p. 28 Eisenhower: "one small ball in the air..." "The President's News Conference of October 9, 1957," John Woolley and Gerhard Peters, The American Presidency Project, University of California, Santa Barbara http://www.presidency.ucsb.edu/ws/index.php?pid=10924; p. 29 Stehling: "It sank..." *Sputnik, the Launch of the Space Race,* Paul Dickson, Macfarlane, Walter, & Ross, Toronto, Ontario, Canada, 2001, p. 156; p. 31 von Braun: "We have firmly established our foothold in space..." "Explorer 1," Franklin O'Donnell, Jet Propulsion Laboratory, California Institute of Technology http://www.jpl.nasa.gov/explorer/downloads/explorer1-textversion.php; Chertok: "However unpleasant..." BBC News: "Sputnik engineer's memories Oct 3, 2007," http://news.bbc.co.uk/player/nol/newsid_7020000/newsid_7026900/7026984.stm?bw=bb&mp=wm&asb=1&news=1&bbcws=1; p. 33 Kennedy: "We choose to go to the moon..." Address about the Nation's Space Effort, delivered at Rice University, Houston, Texas, September 12, 1962. Hear the entire speech at http://www.youtube.com/watch?v=ouRbkBAOGEw; p. 34 Ulam: "how Jules Verne and H. G. Wells had influenced me..." Ulam, p. 5; p. 36 "Mars by 1965,..." *The Curve of Binding Energy,* John McPhee, Farrar, Strauss and Giroux, NY, 1974, p. 180; p. 37 Ulam: "Nuclear energy seems – " "The Future of Nuclear Energy in Space. Conference of the Aerospace Division of the American Nuclear Society," New York City, November 1963. American Philosophical Society Library. Philadelphia, PA; p. 38 von Braun: "If Dr. Ulam is a mathematical wizard..." "The Future of Nuclear Energy in Space. Conference of the Aerospace Division of the American Nuclear Society," New York City, November 1963. Archives, NASA Marshall Space Flight Center. Huntsville, Alabama; Françoise Ulam: "For Stan, Orion meant exploring the universe..." Interview with the author, June 11, 2009, Santa Fe, NM; p. 39 "Funding for nuclear power research..." "Marshall Space Flight Center and the Reactor-in-Flight Stage: A Look Back at Using Nuclear Propulsion to Power Space Vehicles in the 1960s," Mike Wright, NASA Marshall Space Flight Center, Huntsville, Alabama, 2003; p. 41 Armstrong: "Hey Houston...This Saturn gave us a magnificent ride..." "Apollo Expeditions to the Moon, Chapter 11.1." Michael Collins and Edwin E. Aldrin, Jr., http://history.nasa.gov/SP-350/ch-11-1.html; Collins: "The Saturn V rocket which put us in orbit..." ibid., Chapter 11.7; Armstrong: "one small step..." http://www.newsday.com/news/neil-armstrong-quote-from-moon-launched-debate-1.1274680; p. 43 "Where do we go from here?..." *Suddenly Tomorrow Came...A History of the Johnson Space Center,* Henry C. Dethloff, The NASA History Series. Lyndon B. Johnson Space Center, Houston, Texas 1993 p. 203. The full text of the book is provided online in PDF format at http://www.jsc.nasa.gov/history/suddenly_tomorrow/suddenly.htm; p. 44 "All of a sudden..." ibid. p. 211, comment by William R. Kelly; "They understood the necessity..." ibid. p. 242, comment by Henry O. Pohl; p. 49 Reagan: "We can follow our dreams..." Address before a Joint Session of Congress on the State of the Union, Public Papers, January 25, 1986. See also Stuckey, p. 53; p. 57 "rockets still fail..." (Report of the Columbia Accident Investigation Board Volume I NASA p.19 http://caib.nasa.gov/news/report/volume1/default.html; p. 59 Musk: "When I was in college..." CNN Newsroom September 2008, http://transcripts.cnn.com/TRANSCRIPTS/0902/08/cnr.03.html; "make humanity a multi-planet species." "Elon Musk Is Betting His Fortune on a Mission Beyond Earth's Orbit" Carl Hoffman, *Wired* magazine, May 2007; p. 60 Bush: "Returning to the Moon..." "President Bush Announces New Vision for Space Exploration Program," NASA Headquarters, Washington, DC, January 14, 2004; p. 61 McCurdy: "will become it's own destination..." "NASA Plans Permanent Moon Base," Warren E. Leary, *New York Times,* December 5, 2006; p. 62 "Overhead sparkled [the constellation] Orion...." *Wired* magazine, May 2007; p. 63 Musk: "That was frickin' awesome..." "Sweet success at last for Falcon 1 rocket." Stephen Clark, "Spaceflight Now," September 28, 2008, http://spaceflightnow.com/falcon/004/index.html; p. 64 Musk: "the only chance NASA has..." Planetary Society podcast on Feb. 16, 2009, http://www.planetary.org/radio/show/00000328/; "I want to make..." *Wired Magazine,* May 2007; "It will be a long time..." "Aiming for Stars, Entrepreneurs May Also Fill Gaps," Marc Kaufman, *Washington Post,* Washington, DC, September 26, 2008. Additional: Elon Musk conducts online Q&A at WashingtonPost.com: http://spacefellowship.com/2008/09/27/elon-musk-conducts-online-qa-at-washingtonpostcom/; "If the laws of celestial mechanics..." Clarke, *Fountains of Paradise,* p. 47; p. 67 "[They] entangle and hold hands." "Space elevator ... and the next floor is outer space," *Sunday Times:* United Kingdom, January 18, 2009; p. 70 "Hold your hands out to the sun...." Clarke, "Sunjammer," p. 829; pp. 70–71 Montgomery: "The structure is made of aluminum..." "NASA to Attempt Historic Solar Sail Deployment," Science@NASA http://science.nasa.gov/headlines/y2008/26jun_nanosaild.htm; p. 71 von Braun: "The small thrust is effective..." "Ion Propulsion: Over 50 Years in the Making," Mike Wright http://science.nasa.gov/newhome/headlines/prop06apr99_2.htm; p. 72 "Unlike chemical engines..." "Solar Electric (Ion) Propulsion" http://nmp.nasa.gov/ds1/tech/sep.html; pp. 73–74 Rayman: "Dawn communicates with us..." Marc Rayman interview with Christine Holm for *PB&J Magazine,* p. 76 Chang Diaz: "With this technology..." "Transcript: Franklin R. Chang Diaz, Ph.D., Extended Interview. "PBS Wired Science," November 2007 http://www.pbs.org/kcet/wiredscience/story/article/251-transcript_franklin_chang_diaz_extended_interview.html#story; "Future human interplanetary spacecraft..." "Fast, Power-Rich Space Transportation, Key to Human Space Exploration and Survival," Chang Diaz, 53rd International Astronautical Congress, The World Space Congress, Houston, TX, 2002; p. 77 Ulam: "the revolutions... "The Future of Nuclear Energy in Space," Conference of the Aerospace Division of the American Nuclear Society in New York City, 1963, American Philosophical Society Library, Philadelphia, PA; Dyson: "I'm strongly interested..." http://www.youtube.com/watch?v=E3Lxx2VAYI8

ILLUSTRATION CREDITS

Cover and 73, 44, 56 up NASA/KSC; pp. 6, 17, 40, 42, 48, 50, 53, 65, 74 NASA; p. 1 and back cover Shutterstock; pp. 2–3 David Aguilar; p. 8 "Chinese Rockets Repel Mongols—1232" by Charles Hubbell; p.10 *Pages of Perfection. Islamic Paintings and Calligraphy from the Russian Academy of Sciences, St. Petersburg,* Art Restoration for Cultural Heritage. Salzburg-Bergheim, Austria: 1995 p. 203; p. 11 photo taken at Oxford University Museum of Natural History by Andrew Gray; p. 14 Corbis p. 16 USSR postage stamp; pp. 19, 20, 21, 23, 30, 31, 32, 34, 37, 71 NASA/MSFC; p. 22 Imperial War Museum; p. 24 Kenneth Ek, Sweden; pp. 26–27 Sergei Korolyov in VDNH, Ostankino, Moscow; p. 28 NASA/Asif A. Siddiqi; p. 29 photo released by U.S. Navy; p. 35 Los Alamos National Laboratory Photo Archives; p. 39 *Straight Herblock* (Simon and Schuster 1964), by permission of Herb Block Foundation; p. 45 NASA/Johnson Space Center; 47 NASA/Kim Shiflett; p. 52 NASA/Bill Ingalls; p. 55 European Space Agency; p. 56 ctr and Io NASA/ Victor Zelentsov; p. 57 *Newton* magazine, Italy; pp. 58, 63, 68 NASA/Pat Rawlings; p. 60 NASA, Boeing; p. 62 SpaceX; p. 66 Tom Nugent/LaserMotive LLC; p. 67 courtesy Alain Rochefort, École Polytechnique de Montréal; p. 77 Ad Astra.

INDEX

Boldface indicates illustrations.